CONFESSIONS OF A
MUSIC CRITIC

for Maureen

CONFESSIONS OF A
MUSIC CRITIC

CHRISTOPHER MORLEY

BREWIN BOOKS

BREWIN BOOKS
19 Enfield Ind. Estate,
Redditch,
Worcestershire,
B97 6BY
www.brewinbooks.com

Published by Brewin Books 2021

A CIP catalogue record for this book is
available from the British Library.

ISBN: 978-1-85858-726-4

Printed and bound in Great Britain
by Page Bros Ltd.

CONTENTS

ACKNOWLEDGMENTS

There are many people who have been a huge support in my career and they all deserve my deepest gratitude. Special thanks, though, to; Maureen Morley, Fiona Fraser, Terry Grimley, Andrew Jowett, Robert Matthew-Walker, Siva Oke, Mike Spencer and Linda Fowler and the memories of David Brock, Jonathan Daumler-Ford, John Joubert and my parents.

Above all, special thanks to my dear friend and colleague, without whose determined encouragement this book would never have been completed, Stephannie Williams.

FOREWORD

It was an early spring afternoon, the magnolia in the front garden was in full bloom, and I was painting the fence. The telephone rang.

I dashed indoors to answer it and it was Terry Grimley, my good friend and Arts Editor on the Birmingham Post, of which I'd been appointed Chief Music Critic only days previously.

"There's a cultural package in Milan this weekend and they're offering it to us," he said. "Do you want to go?" It seems crazy now, but I shillied and shallied until Maureen, my wife, said of course I must go.

I had no valid passport at the time, but in those days (1988), you could get a temporary passport at the Post Office, so off I went to secure the document. And the next afternoon I found myself on a rather posh Birmingham Executive Airways aeroplane, destined for Milan.

Hard to imagine now, but the seats were arranged in pairs, facing each other across a table, and there were two attractive ladies in the seats opposite me. I was peering into my Filofax, which was embossed with my initials CFM, and eventually I was interrupted by one of these ladies, asking if I was Christopher Morley.

It turned out that she was Liz Mason, press officer for BEA, who was organising the trip, and her colleague was Jill Smithson, her assistant. The whole enterprise was the brainchild of the Milan Chamber of Commerce, who had decided that, as the city was empty at weekends, they wanted to organise cultural visits from all the cities which had direct flight links to Milan, in order to fill their hotels and keep their retail businesses going over a fallow couple of days.

The three of us got on famously, "Three went to Milan", Liz kept saying, and we enjoyed the freshly-cooked meal served to us on the plane (more about that when I get on to my return). On landing we were taken to our hotel, the multi-starred Hotel Michelangelo, where we were soon met by one of the organisers of this massive weekend, who took us out for dinner at one of Milan's exclusive restaurants. We didn't divulge that we'd already eaten on the plane.

Next morning was breakfast and I'd never seen anything like it. There was so much on offer and even Prosecco to drink (I didn't succumb to that until the last morning of my stay there).

There then seemed to be a whirlwind of events, including a press conference broadcast live on regional Italian TV, during which I was interviewed in Italian (more about my Italian links later), and a lunch launching a new perfume called La Scala, of which I bore home a complimentary bottle.

The central event was of course a visit to the opera at La Scala that evening, and wow, what an experience that was! The production was Wagner's Flying Dutchman, an opera I'd never seen before, and I was bowled over by the music, as well as by the performance and production values. Everything was at the highest level imaginable, and the appearance of the Dutchman's ghost ship, growing and growing menacingly as it approached was truly scary.

Walter Weller, whom I was later to get to know very well during his visits as a much-loved guest to the City of Birmingham Symphony Orchestra, was conducting, drawing an amazingly arresting sound from the orchestra, and the Dutchman was played by James Morris, sporting a full-length leather coat (I subsequently found myself a similar one from the local Oxfam shop, and fancied myself as the doomed traveller – I in fact wore it a year later on tour with the Birmingham Bach Choir to Leipzig, Wagner's birthplace).

The whole evening was magical, beginning with a tour of the La Scala Museum, which displayed a lock of what they claimed was Mozart's hair, continuing with the performance, a prosecco in the marbled bar during the interval, and then the cathartic ending as the Dutchman and Senta made their journey together into eternity.

After the opera we were all taken to probably the most exclusive restaurant in Milan, Savini, in the famous Galleria. We were a motley crew of reviewers from various countries, including one (I shall call him M.M. – in fact his name was indeed very similar to Mickey Mouse!) who became a nuisance during the rest of my stay in Milan. The small talk and point-scoring were tiresome, and the food actually not all that brilliant, but eventually Liz, Jill and I found ourselves back at our hotel, where we planned the coverage I was going to write of the whole weekend.

The ladies were going back home the next morning, as they were able to use British Airways flights (I was condemned to remain another day until the Birmingham Executive Airways flight on the Sunday evening). I accompanied them to the airport in the hotel's courtesy bus, then had the day to myself.

There are only three things I can remember about the rest of the day: going to see Leonardo da Vinci's painting of The Last Supper, eating a nice pizza in a back-street restaurant, and being plagued with phone calls from Mickey Mouse. He was an American freelance writer, based in Milan and grabbing any work which came his way; he seemed to think the Birmingham Post would be interested in his offerings, and persisted in pestering me to commission things from him. I can't remember how I put him down, but eventually I did.

On the Sunday morning my cousin Rosanna, who lived in Milan, and her then husband came to collect me after my prosecco breakfast, took me to their apartment where Rosanna cooked a beautiful joint of lamb, he pressed two flagons of home-made wine on me (how was I supposed to travel with those?), and they eventually gave me a lift to the airport for the flight home.

It was a tiny plane, probably only a 24-seater, and there was one South American passenger who was vociferous in his complaints, saying he'd flown all over the world and this was the worst flight he'd ever been on.

"What's his problem?" I asked the stewardess as she served me the most succulent steak, freshly cooked. "Oh, he's as nervous as hell," she said dismissively. "You can always tell."

I could see right through the cockpit as we came in to land, the lights of Birmingham twinkling beckoningly through the windscreen. I was home, and my long stint as Chief Music Critic of the Birmingham Post had well and truly begun.

But how had all this come about?

All profits from this book will be donated to the
Gwyn Williams Bursary Fund, helping young
string players as they build their future.

Chapter 1

HOW IT ALL BEGAN

It was autumn 1969, and I'd recently graduated as a BMus with Honours from the University of Birmingham. Unfortunately the degree wasn't honourable enough, so I was forced to leave the ivory tower in which I'd planned to carry out lifelong research into Mozart, and instead find a job as a teacher.

So I was now acting Head of Music (the incumbent had escaped back into academe for a year) in a Walsall comprehensive school, with no classroom experience on the other side of the desk, and barely able to understand one word in three of what these streetwise Black Country kids were saying.

Music lessons seemed to consist entirely of singing, and one of my fondest memories was of a Friday-afternoon class of fourth-year boys (Year 10 in today's parlance) belting out "Oo is Sylvia" from the bottom of their hobnailed boots, bless their golden hearts.

My girlfriend was still at the University, studying French, and she and I were living in adjacent bedsits in a house in Moseley. We sat in one of them and bedded in the other. One Sunday lunchtime there was a knock at the front door.

Kenneth Dommett was the music critic of the Birmingham Post and loathed by us music students for his ungenerous, nitpicking and obviously – to us – ill-informed reviews. And now here he was, everyone's image of a wannabe intellectual, bearded, overlong thinning hair, strong pebble-lensed glasses, standing sheepishly on my doorstep.

He was seeking an assistant and his friend and near-neighbour in the posh part of Moseley, my beloved final-year tutor the composer John Joubert, had kindly recommended me. That recommendation transformed my whole world, setting me on the path where only now, more than fifty years on, I see myself gradually dwindling the light at the end of the tunnel. Everything I've achieved I owe to John Joubert, and I have been privileged to put my puny talents at the service of publicising his wonderful compositions, not least his extraordinary opera *Jane Eyre*.

Gobsmacked, I gratefully accepted Ken's offer and he gave me my first assignment, which was to review the Prague String Quartet performing for the much-cultivated Birmingham Chamber Music Society at the city's Museum and Art Gallery. He wanted 250 words and instructed me how to contact the copy-desk at the Birmingham Post and dictate my review over the phone. He also vouchsafed to me wise words "you cannot say so-and-so played like a cow without saying *why* they played like a cow".

So there I was, one Saturday evening in the autumn of 1969, theatrically wielding my pen which went into spectacular scribbling action every time I ostentatiously winced at a wrong note. I still have that review, and despite its priggish tone, it ain't half bad.

Ken was a great discoverer of pubs, and most Sunday lunchtimes he would call for me and take me to his latest find. So far as I was concerned they were nothing to get excited about, but as he was paying I was happy to go along, though it usually meant the rest of the day was a blank washout.

He was actually quite an amazing man. Not at all a musician, he determinedly forged his way into reviewing, and became not only music critic on the Birmingham Post but also a reviewer for record magazines. In those days the Birmingham Post used to invite its contributors to do restaurant reviews as well, and Ken was always up for that (and I did the odd one or two, not least many years later when Symphony Hall opened its short-lived Pizza Plaza – I think I went on Classic FM at the end of the evening, talking about that).

Being music critic on the Birmingham Post was not Ken's sole occupation. His day job was working for HM Customs and Excise in an office somewhere near Snow Hill station and after that he would drive off to his reviewing assignments, some of them as far afield as the Royal Opera House at Covent Garden or the English National Opera at London's Coliseum. He once took me to the latter venue for Britten's Gloriana, phoned in his review immediately afterwards, then entertained me and his wife to an Italian meal in a restaurant just around the corner, and subsequently drove home, where we arrived at about 2 o'clock in the morning, his wife having kept him awake by constantly chattering.

There was one huge hiccup during my early days as a critic for the paper. Ken asked me to review a CBSO concert in Birmingham Town Hall, which included a performance of the world's greatest violin concerto, the Beethoven. The renowned soloist was actually not very good on this occasion, and I said so.

Next day I took a party from the school where I was now Head of Music (St Paul's Grammar School in Edgbaston – what a relief to be in a convent school after my Walsall comprehensive) to see a production of Carmen at the Coliseum, a trip organised by British Rail, who were doing wonderful things in those days.

I returned very late that night to find the proverbial had hit the fan. Telephone lines at the Birmingham Post had been red-hot all day, complaining that I had identified the wrong soloist in my review! I had said it was Ralph Holmes, when in fact the guilty party was a violinist with a very similar name. These lapses of memory do occasionally happen with reviewers (I know that other of my colleagues have been equally as guilty of a similar lapse), but they are unforgiveable and the editor of the paper had no choice but to sack me, in order, apart from anything else, to mitigate the legal consequences.

As luck would have it, Ralph Holmes was due to give a recital at the Barber Institute a couple of weeks later, accompanied by the then Professor of Music at Birmingham University, Ivor Keys. I had never taken to Ivor when he arrived as Prof at the start of my final year there, as I had been totally devoted to his predecessor, Anthony Lewis, who had moved on to become Principal of the Royal Academy of Music in London, but Ivor was very kind to me in this matter.

"I'll arrange for you to meet Ralph during the interval," he said, and sure enough, the meeting came about. Ralph Holmes shook my hand warmly and said "Don't worry, Chris, these things happen!" and that was that. Tutto apposto, as we say in Italian (did I say I am half-Italian?).

I walked home on air that night – but I was no longer reviewing for the Birmingham Post. Except that a few weeks later Ken Dommett went to the editor and said words to the effect that look, Chris has learned his lesson and I need him back. The plea worked and I was reinstated!

I have had my odd allocation of hate mail as a result of my reviews. The usual one is "your critic can't have been at the same concert as I was, because...", when the writer thinks they are being so wittily original – and unthinking, because everyone's reaction to a performance is personal, and not necessarily automatically "right". The critic is in a privileged position because his reactions are being put into print (and until very recently being paid to boot), but also with the caveat that those reactions come from a background of learning and experience.

One example of a hostile response during those early years came as the result of my asking provocatively at the end of a review of Handel's Messiah from the City of Birmingham Choir, do we really still need to stand for the Hallelujah Chorus? People, including one of my colleagues at St Paul's, were outraged.

Another amusing bit of feedback happened when I attended a meeting of all the heads of music in Birmingham grammar schools to plan the forthcoming Birmingham Grammar Schools' Music Festival, held annually in Birmingham Town Hall. The major item was always a large-scale choral work, performed by a chorus of selected members from the various school choirs.

One of the works being discussed as a possibility was the Brahms German Requiem, a performance of which I had reviewed the previous weekend, and in my piece I hadn't concealed the fact that I don't much care for it (I'm with George Bernard Shaw on this).

A little chap whose voice tended to be more of a presence than his stature was sitting opposite me, and piped up sarcastically, "Oh, we can't do the Brahms. Christopher Morley of the Birmingham Post doesn't like it!" I smiled across the table at him. He didn't know it was me.

It can't be helped that we all have blind spots about certain works of art, and in music I have problems with much of Brahms (though I adore his piano concertos, three of the four movements of the Fourth Symphony, the St Anthony Variations, the Academic Festival Overture, and all the chamber works for clarinet). Another bete noir is Carmen, as well as its near-namesake, Carmina Burana.

Ironically, the work chosen for the forthcoming Birmingham Grammar Schools' Music Festival was indeed Carmina Burana and I was asked to train the children's chorus for their two appearances. On the day of the dress rehearsal and performance I hoofed it down to Vincent's wonderful record shop in Needless Alley, just off New Street and treated myself to the Toscanini recording of the Verdi Requiem, so that I could listen to some truly great choral music when I got home that evening. I think it was on that occasion that we had to evacuate the Town Hall during rehearsal because of a bomb scare (it was the time of the Irish troubles).

I should point out, though, that whatever difficulties we critics might have about particular works, we always review their performance objectively. I think it's only when we are reviewing a new work that we can put on record our own reactions to the piece itself (which was what Shaw was doing with the Brahms). I know I've contradicted myself here, but I wrote that review nearly 50 years ago, and have acquired a certain wisdom since.

There was one particularly piquant incident during my early years both as a schoolteacher and as a music critic. Ken sent me to review a Christmas concert from the Birmingham Schools' Music Service (or whatever it was called in those far-off days). Stanley Adams, the city's Music Advisor was conducting, and the programme included a setting by him of the medieval carol Torches.

My review of the concert commented on the fact that Adams' Torches resembled so closely the famous setting by John Joubert, and I wondered which had come first...

Next morning, Sister Josephine, the amazing Headmistress at St Paul's (a Ph.D in English, who was banned by her Mother Superior from watching controversial television plays in the convent, as she lamented to me) received an irate phone call from Mr Adams, demanding she sack me for being so insubordinate.

"Mr Adams," she coolly replied, "I have no influence over what Mr Morley does in his own time," and put the phone down.

A few months later I was due to end my two years as a probationary teacher, and needed to be assessed in classroom action. Who should come to sit in judgement but none other than Stanley Adams!

He stayed and observed three consecutive lessons, which apparently was quite a compliment (if you're obvious rubbish, they can't wait to get away). And I passed my probation, going on to rise through the salary scales, first at St Paul's and subsequently at the Earls High School in Halesowen, where I eventually ended my schoolteaching career.

But while all of this was going on, things had been happening at the Birmingham Post. The people upstairs (those suits who seem to have all the say) had decided that the paper no longer needed a freelance Chief Music Critic, and that they could find one in-house from their own salaried staff.

So they decided that their Business Editor, who had once been to a few concerts in Liverpool, would take over and Ken Dommett was given the push.

An awkward Saturday night followed and I think I have got the sequence of events right, though this was nearly 50 years ago. I went to review a concert (Midland Youth Orchestra?) and then met Ken and Irene, his wife, in some nearby pub, where they put the thumbscrews on me not to continue writing for the newspaper which had treated Ken so shamefully.

After that I went on into the offices of the Birmingham Post, very late at night, to meet the new Chief Music Critic, who tried very hard to impress me with the concerts he'd been to, and how he looked forward to working with me. I departed, unconvinced.

I wrote to the Editor, resigning, saying that I could no longer work for a newspaper which treated its contributors in the way it had treated Ken. He replied, saying that he wished I had consulted with him to find out the true facts before making my decision.

And that was that. I was no longer a permanent music critic. Would I make such a Quixotic gesture now? No, of course I wouldn't. But half-a-century ago, in my idealistic innocence, I thought that was the honourable way forward.

Chapter 2

THE WILDERNESS YEARS

Ken and I had worked very well together during those few years. In my naivety, I didn't realise then how much he was relying on me for well-informed backup. I can see that now and remain flattered that he should have needed me so much.

There was only one occasion when I sensed a glimmer of what our relationship was all about, and that was when the world premiere of Shostakovich's 15th Symphony was broadcast live from Moscow in 1972, conducted by the composer's son Maxim.

Ken invited me round to his house to listen to this relay. It was a Sunday lunchtime and of course a bottle of Nicolas (the wine of the 1970s) had been opened (there was always a bottle chambre-ing in the hearth). We settled down for the performance.

As it progressed I came out with the insights Ken was obviously hoping I'd make: these were the references to fallen heroes (William Tell, Wagner's Siegfried and Tristan), the ticking percussion (though at that point, never having heard the work, I didn't realise that was a reference to Shostakovich's long-suppressed Fourth Symphony).

He duly sent in his review and it is a tribute to the Birmingham Post of those days that the newspaper wanted to cover reviews of major artistic events, wherever in the world. My first review as Chief Music Critic many years later was of a CBSO concert conducted by Simon Rattle in, I think San Francisco, relayed live on BBC2 and instantly covered by the Birmingham Post (a reader complained that I wrote too much about Rattle's facial expressions and I replied that this was in fact a television relay I was reviewing!).

The paper was a major force in the arts world in those days and its name remains so even now, which is why I still have the entree to so many events internationally.

A major event I covered during my time working for Ken was the UK premiere of Prokofiev's War and Peace at the Coliseum in London. This was a massively important occasion. David Lloyd Jones was the conductor, Norman Bailey, fresh from his recent triumph as Hans Sachs in Sadler's Wells' Mastersingers played General Kutuzov, and Josephine Barstow sang Natasha. Her New Year's Ball scene lives still in my memory.

I think this was the latest deadline extension I ever had and I dictated my review at about 11.15 that evening from one of those hooded telephone kiosks at Euston Station, before hopping onto the last train to Birmingham. And the review was in the paper next morning.

That was always a thrill, seeing what I'd written appearing in print a few hours later. I remember once reviewing a concert, phoning in the review, dashing home for a couple of hours' sleep and then making my way to Birmingham Airport for a flight to Italy on family business. At Birmingham International I bought a copy of the Birmingham Post in the very early hours, and there was my review.

*   *   *

But with the sacking of Ken Dommett and my idealistic resignation in support, I now found myself in the wilderness as a reviewer. I had become used to having the entree to musical events and felt the need to continue as a presence on the Midlands musical scene.

For a while I scrabbled a weekly column on the Birmingham Evening Mail, whose editorial staff were very kind to me. In that column I tried to squeeze in as many references as I could into a few hundred words, so there was a brief comment about the premiere of the Leonard Bernstein Mass relayed on television, Alfred Brendel playing Mozart piano concertos at the Cheltenham Festival, a whole week at that year's Hereford Three Choirs Festival, and all kinds of other things.

I can't remember why that fragile existence came to an end, but it did. For a while after that there was nothing, until someone I'd known only slightly at Birmingham University rang me. She was the Birmingham correspondent of the respected magazine Music and Musicians, and was now leaving the area for a teaching post at Queen's University, Belfast and would I like to take over from her?

Of course I jumped at the offer. This involved a lengthy column every three months, rounding up everything I'd heard, and it was a joy to produce. It meant I could once again claim complimentary admittance to CBSO concerts (where the wonderful and still nowadays disgracefully under-rated Louis Fremaux was in charge), all the other major events going on in Birmingham, and to operatic presentations at Birmingham Hippodrome from English National Opera (Mastersingers, the Ring among the highlights) and Welsh National Opera.

One of my visits to the Hippodrome for a WNO production had an amazing outcome. It was a performance of La Traviata (I think the wonderful Suzanne Murphy was singing Violetta), and the company manager made his apologetic way through the curtain to tell us that the tenor (someone I didn't rate anyway) was unwell and the part of Alfredo would be taken by Dennis O'Neill.

Who was this Dennis O'Neill? By the time the performance ended I certainly wanted to know! His tone was so mellifluous, his phrasing so shapely, his power so present but so unforced, and I was determined to congratulate him. So for the first and only time in my life I made my way to the stage door and talked my way into his dressing-room.

"You reminded me of Pavarotti," I said. He replied, "I'm so moved," and thanked me for making the effort to come backstage and find him. Next morning I rang the editor of Music and Musicians (Keith Clarke, who has become a dear friend – more of him later when I talk about Walton's La Mortella villa in Ischia), to tell him that he simply had to make some stop-press space available for me to rave about this young tenor – and he did.

Music and Musicians was part of the Hansom Books stable, which came to an unfortunate end, as did the six other companion magazines, Dance and Dancers, Books and Bookmen, Plays and Players among them. The owner simply couldn't afford to keep it all running anymore and took the only available way out as it seemed to him – suicide.

Keith Clarke did his valiant best to keep the enterprise going for a while, but it had to come to an end. At the denouement all the contributors to the various magazines were left being owed massive sums in fees, which we never received. I remember on one occasion Keith's predecessor as Editor spotted me at an Association of British Orchestras event in London, could sense that I was about to buttonhole him about all the money owing me, and promptly scuttled into a lift which was going in the opposite direction from mine.

So, yet again, no writing outlet, until there came another serendipitous phone call.

The caller identified himself as Malcolm McGivan, editor of Arts Report, a monthly newspaper published by West Midlands Arts, an organisation certainly to be reckoned with in the 1980s. Malcolm had been given my name by Terry Grimley and asked me if I would like to write a feature each month for his newspaper.

This was in fact something quite prestigious and of course I took it on. Those were heady times and I reviewed major events both in the Midlands and elsewhere when local organisations were involved. One such occasion was the debut of Jeffrey Skidmore's Ex Cathedra at St John's Smith Square in London. I travelled on the coach with the chamber choir and on the way back, late at night, Terry Grimley (who had come on the trip to review for the Birmingham Post) and I probably irritated the dozing choristers by "Naming That Tune" to each other; I seem to remember most of his tunes were by the Danish composer Carl Nielsen, one of Terry's many obsessions.

There was also space for record reviews and the first one I ever undertook was Ex Cathedra's first recording, an LP of Christmas music and one which I reviewed rather pretentiously, noting every crackle on the surface of the disc. I established a great relationship with the aforementioned Vincent's record shop in Needless Alley, who would supply me with LPs and cassettes (a medium which had just come in and which I still find very convenient to this day) of recordings by locally-based performers, including, naturally, the CBSO.

One important assignment I undertook for Arts Report was going down to the Royal Academy of Music in London to interview the composer Sir Michael Tippett (one of my idols) in his 80th birthday year. Once again Terry was with me, but he left it to me to ask all the technical questions (shades again of Ken Dommett from nearly two decades earlier). Tippett rewarded me by signing my score of his Fantasia Concertante on a Theme of Corelli, a work for string orchestra which I absolutely adore.

Liz Griffin, editor of the Malvern Gazette (Tippett was due to conduct the English Symphony Orchestra in Malvern later in the year), should have been there but she arrived late as her train had been delayed, so Terry and I filled her in about the interview in the RAM coffee bar and virtually wrote her copy for her.

Liz and her husband David, who actually worked on the Birmingham Post, though I didn't know that at the time, have remained dear colleagues, as has Terry Grimley. Malcolm McGivan and I were very close friends for a while, though we eventually lost touch.

But the most significant occurrence during this period in the wilderness years was a press conference announcing the appointment of a new principal conductor of the CBSO. There was a huge intake of breath when we heard how old this person was: only 25. And there was a buzz of excitement when we were told his name, recent winner of the John Player Conducting Competition in Bournemouth.

His name was Simon Rattle.

Chapter 3

MY BEGINNINGS

I owe my existence to an Austro-Bavarian housepainter and an Italian autocrat. Had Hitler and Mussolini not strutted their stuff across Europe and North Africa I wouldn't be here.

Frank Morley, a young Post Office clerk in Brighton, was called up to serve in the British Army during World War II, and after training in Catterick, he embarked from Liverpool in a naval convoy heading south. At the Straits of Gibraltar the convoy split, half heading on to the Cape of Good Hope and then on into the Indian Ocean and the horrors of the war with the Japanese, the other half turned left into the Mediterranean and landed in Algeria. Frank was in that half.

As part of Montgomery's Eighth Army, they made their way across North Africa, then sailed across the Mediterranean, arriving eventually in Naples. Safely ensconced there as liberators, the British Army requisitioned a beautiful villa in the peaceful and somewhat patrician suburb of Vomero, at the top of the hill so famous in all the postcards, overlooking the bay, and Frank set to work there, arranging transport (armoured cars, tanks, chauffeured vehicles).

They needed secretarial staff, so it was made public that jobs were available to local residents and the 18-year-old Bice Pilla applied and landed a job. She was pretty and lively, but had no secretarial skills, so the officers themselves did all her typing for her.

Everyone seemed to be enchanted by her except one shy, tall, blond, good-looking young man, who kept his distance – Frank. Bice was piqued and intrigued that, unlike the others, he was keeping himself aloof.

One evening the telephone rang in Bice's apartment, the home she shared with her brother and three sisters (their parents had died very young). It was from one of the soldiers at the villa, who spoke a bit of Italian.

"I have a message from Frank Morley," he said. "Would you like to go to the opera with him?"

And Bice agreed. The British Army always had complimentary tickets to the newly re-opened San Carlo Opera house in Naples and Frank and Bice's first date was to go there to see Arrigo Boito's Mefistofele.

It must have been a whirlwind romance, because that production was premiered on February 1 1946 (I have the history of the San Carlo which tells me so), and they were married on August 5 of that year. Bice was 19 and Frank 22.

Frank was later moved, garrisoned elsewhere in Italy, and eventually back to England in Woking, preparing for demobilisation. Bice, now an army wife and automatically a British citizen, received food parcels delivered weekly from the Quartermaster, for which her family, after so many wartime privations were deeply thankful to her, and eventually just before Christmas in 1946, made the long train journey to England (a very meandering route after the destruction of so many railway lines in Europe) and settled into digs which Frank had found for her in London, I think in Maida Vale.

It was during the cold, snowbound winter of 1947, and Mum and Dad must have been snuggling up very close to keep warm on one of his weekend leaves when I was conceived early that January.

After Dad's demobilisation and return to the Post Office they moved to Brighton and the house Dad's mother was renting (his father had died long ago). They lived on the ground floor, his mother upstairs, and I was born that October.

There was always music in the house, Mum singing Neapolitan songs, and the most gorgeous lullabies to me (and all my bedtime stories and prayers were in Italian), Dad playing his collection of 78s, including Delius' La Calinda (which still makes me feel wistful, and I treasure that original disc to this day), Tchaikovsky's Capriccio Italien (the opening of which used to scare me), Debussy's Clair de Lune played by the Andre Kostelanetz Orchestra (Ravel's Pavane pour une Infante Defunte on the back), and Rossini's Thieving Magpie Overture.

Family legend has it that I used to conduct the crescendo of that overture when I was two, and that at the same age I used to sing La Donna e Mobile from Verdi's Rigoletto. I know for a fact that when I had just turned 5 I was selected to sing O Little Town of Bethlehem as a solo at my infants' school Carol Service (Mum, who was just about to give birth to my brother Aldo, said I looked so red in the face she thought I was going to explode), and two years later I was cast as King Herod in the nativity play, wanting to kill all the children. In view of my nickname of "Mr Death", many years later as a schoolteacher, perhaps that was quite prescient (don't get me wrong, I actually loved my pupils; I was just very firm with them, and they appreciated that).

When I was six I was put to the piano, as the expression goes, and progressed pretty well, eventually winning prizes at the Brighton Competitive Music Festival, including a cup for sight-reading (a skill I'd developed through never doing much practising between lessons).

As I grew older, music became an increasingly important element in my life. There was a wonderful, Dickensian secondhand bookshop in Brighton (Holleyman and Treacher, of blessed memory), which had an amazing music department. I used to haunt it a lot and bought much piano music and many orchestral and vocal scores there. A great find there many years later was a miniature leather-bound score on the finest India paper of Wagner's Parsifal, signed by Elgar's muse, Alice Stuart-Wortley, who bought it in Bayreuth in 1908.

I was so lucky to have a lovely, safe, secure family, and to attend schools which I really loved. And it was Audrey Cheffings, the music teacher at my beloved Westlain Grammar School, who was the unwitting engineer of my Damascene moment.

She had a contact with links to Glyndebourne Festival Opera, not very far at all from Westlain, both establishments nestling in the South Downs. One lovely June morning at the end of my Fifth Year, O-levels all over, she took our small music group to Glyndebourne for one of the final rehearsals of Mozart's Idomeneo, an opera about which I knew nothing.

To say I was bowled over would be an understatement. Walking through the beautiful grounds, past the tennis courts, on such a gorgeous early summer's day was wondrous enough, but then entering the auditorium to be greeted by such amazing music was to be knocked for six.

This was a costume rehearsal just prior to dress rehearsal, with full orchestra, so it was very close to a real performance. John Pritchard was conducting the London Philharmonic Orchestra (in his autobiography he later took against a review I'd written of one of his Prom concerts), Gundula Janowitz, looking absolutely ravishing, was singing Ilia's aria "Se il padre perdei" with wonderful woodwind obbligati, and the rest of the cast included Richard Lewis, a very thin Luciano Pavarotti, still comparatively unknown in this country, and David Hughes, the Birmingham-born pop star who had been so desperate to cross over into the world of opera, and who sadly died of heart disease very soon after he made that breakthrough.

I was entranced and couldn't speak. We went back to school in time for lunch, but I couldn't bear to socialise in the canteen. Instead, I took myself off into the school library, ruled some staves in an exercise-book, and tried to write down and fix as much as I could of the shattering music I'd heard that morning (I still have that exercise-book).

The die was cast, and it could only be music from that time on.

A year later (we are now in the summer of 1965) I was offered the chance of a place on a three-week course in Music and German in Salzburg. The cost was £50.00 and Dad said he would match any grant I was offered by the Brighton Education Committee.

They offered me £12/10shillings (£12.50 in today's devalued currency), which would have totalled £25.00 with Dad's contribution. So I wrote back, thanking them for their offer, but saying it was no use to me unless they doubled it. And they did! They must have admired my sixth-form cheek.

As I set off on my journey I opened a letter Dad had given me, to be read only when I was en route. "This is your first trip abroad on your own," he said. "Remember you are representing your country, and don't let me down." Those sentiments might now sound stiff and pious, but I took them to heart.

Salzburg was amazing. To be in the city where Mozart was born, to see all the sights he had seen, to visit the churches in which his music had been performed, was intoxicating. There were free concerts at the Mozarteum every night (I remember one evening when a bat was fluttering around the ceiling; "What a pity they're not doing Die Fledermaus," wagged one of the many new-found friends I made).

And they were indeed wonderful new friends, many of whom I kept up with for several years. One was Peter Hunt, for whom I composed a piece for French Horn and strings, premiered by him at his school, Wellington College (socially rather a cut above Westlain Grammar School). I paid a visit to his rather exclusive family home once, at Sutton in Surrey, and that evening Peter and I went to the pictures, driven at breakneck speed through the Surrey lanes by his elder brother, James. Yes, James Hunt, who later became a world-famous Grand Prix racing-driver.

Next day I went on to West Norwood, to stay with the greatest friend I made in Salzburg, Diana Ashcroft, who remains one of my closest friends to this day. Over the next couple of years she and I attended many important concerts in London, including the London premiere of Britten's Songs and Proverbs of William Blake at the Fairfield Halls (the composer accompanying the great baritone Dietrich Fischer-Dieskau; the programme also included the Mozart Clarinet Quintet with Gervase de Peyer and the Amadeus String Quartet – that's your signature tune, she said), a powerful Britten War Requiem at the Royal Albert Hall, though we also bunked off a Beethoven Nine conducted by Sir Malcolm Sargent as the traditional penultimate Prom concert of the season in order to go to the cinema to see The Fall of the Roman Empire.

Diana is now the wife of John de la Cour, a scion of the Beauchamp family, with strong links with Madresfield Court at the foot of the Malvern Hills. Together they run the grant-giving Elmley Foundation, funding musical projects in Worcestershire and Herefordshire.

So my Salzburg experience reinforced in me the conviction that my life had to be devoted to music, but my teachers at Westlain didn't agree. Both the heads of French (who was also the formidable Deputy Headmistress) and German were determined that I should study their languages, probably at Oxford.

They both gave me so much of their own time to cram me after school with extra tuition, both bringing me great works of literature in their respective languages to study, and I remain eternally grateful to them for their overwhelming interest in me.

But I was unhappy. I wanted to immerse myself in music and all that a university education in the subject could offer. I went to the Headmaster, Cyril Ferguson, a wonderful man who had worked in Bomb Disposal during the War, and who, like me had a stammer, which he overcame every morning to deliver School Assembly.

"Sir, I'm so grateful for what Miss Berry and Mrs Berry-Richards are doing for me, but I really want to do Music at university," I blurted. He listened, and then came out with an astonishing reply "I need to see a reference from someone to confirm that you're up to it, and if I see that, then I'll support you all the way."

I obtained that reference, from John Parry, who had been one of the tutors in Salzburg, and who wrote me the most glowing testimonial. Mr Ferguson accepted it, and I proceeded with my university applications.

Scouring the prospectuses, I found that the University of Birmingham was offering Open Entrance Scholarships worth £100 per year to new under-graduates, and I liked the sound of the Music Department there. I duly applied, was called for interview and a whole couple of days built around the applicants for those Scholarships.

It was a wonderful, heady couple of days, culminating in my interview with the Scholarship Board, headed by Richard Hoggart, he of the amazing book which had turned the class-world on its head, *The Uses of Literacy*. I answered various technical, searching questions, and then came the killer question, from Hoggart himself.

"Why do you want this Scholarship?" I suspect he was expecting some mealy-mouthed, platitudinous claptrap, but instead I responded, "Because I could do with the money". "That's a bloody good answer," he said.

A few days later a bulky letter arrived for me back home in Brighton and I opened it with trepidation. I had been awarded the Scholarship! As I told my parents I jumped up and down and nearly hit my head on our low bungalow ceiling.

I immediately rang Mr Ferguson at his home in Lewes and he was overjoyed. Westlain was a new school, and I was the first student to obtain an Open Entrance Scholarship to university. "Come to the front of the Hall for tomorrow's Assembly," he instructed. And there he informed the school of my achievement and I was warmly congratulated, not least by my lovely sixth-form friends.

Chapter 4

THE UNIVERSITY YEARS

My final two terms at Westlain were heady, as I knew I was now firmly launched on the path I had chosen for myself. Audrey Cheffings assembled a school orchestra, for which I composed a Westlain March, conducting its premiere at Speech Day that Spring. She coached me for a successful pass in Music 'S'-level (I doubt that qualification still exists), in which the work set for close study was the Piano Concerto in D minor K466 by my now beloved Mozart; and after the exam period we put on our first-ever school opera, Gilbert and Sullivan's Trial by Jury, in which I took the part of Edwin, the caddish Defendant.

For some reason I was given a powder-blue Regency frock-coat to wear. I took it home to acclimatise myself to it, and really fancied myself wearing it and looking like Haydn in a famous painting. So much so, in fact, that one Saturday morning I wore it as I composed a Nocturnal for guitar (Britten had just written a Nocturnal for the guitarist Julian Bream) for a new friend I had recently made, Brian Agate in the Lower Sixth.

Brian had a younger sister, Linda, who sang Angelina in Trial by Jury. She was the lust object of many of the post-pubescent boys in the school, and I was the envy of all of them when I was paired with her for the staff v. school tennis match that year – and we won.

The conductor of the show, with two pianos played by his wife and Mrs Cheffings, was the Head of Biology, the appropriately-named Alan Skull, who had instilled in me during the previous couple of years enthusiasms for Mahler, Bruckner and Berg (we used to share bargain LPs we had unearthed of music by those composers).

After a rapturous reception at the end of the opening night we all went over the busy A27 Brighton to Lewes road, to the Swan at Falmer, which had long been the Sixth-Formers' local. I remember Mr Ferguson and Geoff Sears, my form-tutor falling out over who was to have the honour of buying me the first drink (stout and cider, the poor man's Black Velvet)!

Eventually came the last day of term and the end of my time at the school I had loved so much, and which had given me so many opportunities. Though I was looking forward so much to breaking away from home and launching my career, I realised I was finding it difficult to leave this building where I had spent seven happy, fulfilling years. I hung around, haunting the corridors and classrooms, until about 5 o'clock, and then went to knock on Mr Ferguson's door.

"Sir, I want to thank you for everything the school has given me," I said. "I'm finding it so difficult to tear myself away."

He came round his desk and shook my hand. "The very best of luck, Chris – and one word of advice: watch the lunchtime drinking!" Our Sixth-Form sorties across the fields to the Swan had obviously not gone un-noticed.

*   *   *

Life at the University of Birmingham was all and more than I'd hoped it would be. The lectures were so involving, the tutorials were stimulating, the concert-life was invigorating.

The professional concerts in the jewel which is the Barber Institute were world-class (early on I heard the renowned Borodin String Quartet there), our own Musical Society concerts were exceptional (my first-ever event with the UMS was that first Christmas – 1966 – singing tenor in the chorus for the Bach Magnificat and Honegger's Christmas Cantata, both works which have ever since meant so much to me, though the Honegger is so rarely performed). And there were also Club Nights every Friday, when students could present their own programmes, and where I precociously very early on led sight-reading performances of Britten's Simple Symphony and Hymn to St Cecilia. And then it was always straight to the Gun Barrels, the pub down the road.

Many happy times were spent in the Barrels, cementing friendships forged through everyone's deep commitment to music and to each other in this wonderful Music Department. It was an iconic place for us all, and years later, when the Barrels was demolished in order to give way to a hideous new building, I drove there to collect some shattered remnants of the Gents' lavatory (where I used to return so much of the Brew XI I had rented), which I placed in my rockery, along with bits of the old Snow Hill railway station.

My first year in the department was even more rewarding than I'd ever hoped for, and I felt that I'd become a small part of that wonderful community of academics, composers, and such talented students – and they had all embraced me!

The long vacation came, bringing a return to Brighton, a place I really didn't want to be anymore. I was spending all day alone at home, Dad out at work, Aldo at school, and Mum away with her sisters in Naples. All I could do was sit and brood, missing my life at Birmingham and increasingly terrified that all of them there would forget me, and I would never be able to pick up the pieces when I returned.

Things became very black. Everything I thought of turned into horrible distortions. I browsed my favourite bookshop, picked up a copy of Jean-Paul Sartre's *La Nausee*, and realised I didn't dare read that exposition of nihilism. I went to the doctor, but he refused to prescribe me anti-depressants, telling me I could get through this on my own. I went to Confession and the priest said "Let your head rule your heart".

Two things got me through this abyss. Tove Jansson's wonderful, simplistic, life-affirming *Moomintroll* stories and late Beethoven string quartets, especially Op.127 in E-flat.

I made a couple of trips back to Birmingham during that long vac, and they certainly helped, making me realise I had not been forgotten. Everything improved and as my second year began, I was back on track.

There had been one particular highlight of my first year, when Anthony Lewis, my beloved Professor, had invited his own beloved teacher, the great and esteemed Nadia Boulanger, over to Birmingham to conduct the University Chorus and the CBSO in the Requiem by Faure, her own beloved teacher.

Prof prepared us in weekly choral rehearsals, and then the exciting evening arrived when we were to be conducted in the final piano rehearsal by Boulanger herself.

This tiny old lady entered the room and we stood and applauded, awestruck to be in the presence of someone who had been the teacher of practically every great composer of the 20th century, from Stravinsky onwards, and who herself had learned her craft from Gabriel Faure. We were becoming part of musical history.

She addressed us. "You, my formidable young friends, have so much strength in you. You will see things that I will never see. Thank you for inviting me."

But she was the formidable one, with more strength in her little finger than all of us put together. We were all tremendously moved, even the hard-boiled brass players who were singing in the choir for this special occasion, and gave her our all. It proved to be an unforgettable performance in Birmingham Town Hall, and I don't think any of us privileged to have taken part have ever got over it.

Now I was in my second year and I really felt my feet were now safely under the table. I had made many friends of both sexes (we were all in fact like a big family of siblings and were so supportive of each other), with two particularly close ones, both violinists: Roland Fudge, a year older than me, with whom I was sharing a flat, and Jonathan Taylor, leader of the Midland Youth Orchestra (he played the Bruch G minor Concerto with them, on a Stradivarius loaned to him, and I so enjoyed being his rehearsal accompanist), and an expert viola-player, too. It was always my dream to conduct a performance of the wonderful Mozart Sinfonia Concertante with Roland solo violin and Jonathan solo viola, but Roland was already busy working for his Finals.

Jonathan later became leader of the Bournemouth Symphony Orchestra, and Roland spent more and more of his time as a composer of community-targeted music.

During the autumn term Anthony Lewis put on a concert performance of Beethoven's only opera, Fidelio (our operatic set work for intensive study), with a cast of soloists including some from Welsh National Opera's then current production. I was in the prisoners' chorus.

During the afternoon rehearsal, as the crucial liberation fanfare moment approached, with an offstage trumpet up in the wings, high above the Barber Institute's orchestra pit, Prof Lewis put down his baton.

"I need someone to go up there and bring in the trumpet. Morley, you do it!"

To say I felt thrilled to be singled out by the Prof for this honour would be an understatement. I dashed up to the wings offstage, positioned myself where I could look down at the pit onto the Prof, and in sight of my friend Derek Glendinning, the trumpeter.

The rehearsal resumed and the crucial moment came, Fidelio/Leonora declaiming "Und du bist tot!", all action to be cut short by the sounding of the fanfare. I anticipated the Prof's downbeat perfectly, bringing Derek in at exactly the right time, and his trumpet resounded across the Barber auditorium. Derek, for all he was an athlete as well as a trumpeter, actually lacked a little in self-confidence, and I think he was glad that the Prof had sent someone up there to help.

Between the rehearsal and the performance I dashed back on the Outer Circle bus to our flat in Rotton Park to collect my conductor's baton. No, I didn't really need it, as hand gestures would have sufficed, but I wanted to add to the sense of occasion. It all went triumphantly and Derek bought me a pint that night in, of course, the Gun Barrels.

I have so many wonderful memories of the Barber Institute: the calm of its atmosphere, its amazing Art Gallery, the Art Library where I sometimes used to escape in order to work in solitude whenever the lovely Music Library became too congenial with bonhomie, but above all, the concert hall, which to this day remains a joy to enter.

In those days, over half-a-century ago, all students were on a three-line whip to attend the celebrity evening concerts, not that we needed any coercion, with so many world-class performers appearing before us. Maggie Costello, the Music Department secretary, had the task of allocating tickets to us for these concerts, and she used to make it her business to keep tabs on who was going out with whom, so that she could allocate seats together. Funny how she always knew...

My fondest memories of the Barber, though, are of taking the stage there as a performer. A certain number of the Friday lunchtime concerts (always preceded by a wonderful buffet lunch down in the dungeons) were allotted to students. To my huge surprise, Adrian Carpenter, a tenor I'd palled up with almost immediately after we arrived at university as First-years, asked me to conduct in the concert he'd successfully applied for. He himself was going to conduct a Handel Organ Concerto, but he wanted me to conduct Warlock's Capriol Suite, which of course I did with huge enthusiasm.

The Easter term of 1968 ended with my own lunchtime concert, in which I conducted some small-scale choral works by Faure, using a particular method of shaping phrases I had learnt from Nadia Boulanger during that unforgettable Faure Requiem of a year earlier, and Schubert's Fifth Symphony, into whose first movement I inserted a couple of silent bars after the exposition in order to let the flautist page-turn comfortably before her crucial entry at the start of the development section.

Mum and Dad had left Brighton at around 6am that morning to drive up for the concert, bringing a tape-recorder (a full-scale reel-to-reel machine, long before the days of cassette recorders), which Kenneth Wilkins, the music librarian, showed them how to plug into a socket in the auditorium floor, and somewhere I still have the recording they made.

At the end of the concert, after introducing Mum and Dad to some of my friends (not least one whom I was coaching in songs by Faure – that composer again), we drove back down to Brighton for the Easter vacation. What a long day at the wheel for Dad. It was the end of a hugely exciting term for me, but there was much more to come that summer, including one spectacularly significant encounter.

* * *

The major feature of the spring term was always the Barber Opera, a tradition launched by Anthony Lewis in the late 1950s, and which by the mid-60s had become internationally-renowned, with reviews in the major national newspapers and BBC broadcasts. Prof was a great baroque conductor and these operas featured works by Scarlatti, Rameau and particularly Handel. The one non-baroque exception was Haydn and his Orfeo, the opera he composed for performance during one of his London visits in the 1790s, but which had never been seen in England until this production in 1967. I was in the chorus for that, as well as manoeuvring the authentic backdrops under Roland's tutelage.

I also remember having the temerity to offer a word of advice to the lovely Rae Woodland, the famous New Zealand soprano who was singing the part of Sybil. She had to deliver a fiendish coloratura aria, going up to the E three ledger lines above the stave and seemed to be having difficulties. "Think you're going up to F-sharp," I said (a tip I'd been taught by Audrey Cheffings when I was singing Edwin in Trial by Jury).

That night Rae came offstage having sung the aria brilliantly. When she spotted me in the wings she smiled me a huge thumbs-up and said "F-sharp!"

In 1968 it was a return to Handel for what was sadly to be the Prof's last Barber Opera. This was Admeto, starring Janet Baker, whose career Anthony Lewis had done so much to advance (his recording of Purcell's Dido and Aeneas, with her in the title role, still remains unsurpassable). I was given the title of assistant stage manager and was also entrusted with the responsibility of ensuring that Janet was given all her props (swords, daggers and suchlike).

She was a joy to work with and I plucked up the courage to ask her to sign an LP of her singing Schumann's Frauenliebe und Leben (Martin Isepp accompanying), which she did, with a beautiful inscription. Of course I still treasure that disc.

Later that term it was Orchestral Dance time, when all final-year undergraduates had to submit a piece of orchestration, either an original composition (which it usually was) or a transcription of a standard work (which it generally wasn't), to be performed by the University Orchestra in a public concert at the Barber.

The audience was all assembled, waiting for this intriguing concert to begin. But it didn't. An important member of the orchestra had been delayed, so we couldn't start. Roland, Jonathan and I started to grumble, but then came up with a brilliant idea.

Somehow we produced a miniature score of the Bach Concerto for Two Violins (whether from one of their violin cases, or from me dashing into the music library I can't remember), I placed it on the music-stand of the piano at the side of the stage, and the three of us launched into an impromptu performance of that fabulous piece which kept the audience occupied and indeed entranced, as their applause at the end indicated. After that, the concert itself seemed a bit of an anticlimax!

Another of the Friday lunchtime student concerts was organised by the brilliant Brian Fieldhouse, a self-deprecating genius, who decided to put on a performance of Walton's Facade, and he asked me to play percussion. During that year I had made it my business to teach myself percussion in order to gain orchestral experience, and I think I must have been pretty successful in order to be able carry out the searching demands of the Walton.

We had such fun preparing and performing that extraordinary work my aforementioned friend Adrian Carpenter and Ilona Sekacz (who had conned the examiners at the end of the first year by writing a learned treatise on a non-existent song-cycle by Richard Rodney Bennett and who later became a prominent composer of incidental music, not least for the Royal Shakespeare Company) were the reciters, standing each one side of the stage beside loudspeakers relaying the other one's voice, and we musicians were flamboyantly dressed. I wore an hallucinatory psychedelic shirt, one of Marks and Spencers' finest. It all went down a storm.

As the end of term and the end of my second year approached I was arranging a performance of Beethoven's Choral Fantasia which I was going to conduct in the magnificent Great Hall. Gary Peacock, boyfriend of one of my closest friends (indeed, she had put me up during one of my returns to Birmingham during my depression of the previous summer) in the department, was the piano soloist, and he was perfect for the improvisatory, almost slapdash qualities of the long solo piano introduction. I assembled a choir and six vocal soloists as well as an orchestra, some of whom came up back from London, where they were now settled, and we had a great time.

The audience loved it, perhaps glad to have heard such a rare, eccentric piece by such a great composer and as we left, John Joubert congratulated me on the way I had managed the many difficult pauses.

My second year at Birmingham University had finished on a high, but the highest high was yet to come during the ensuing long vacation (and what a contrast from my depression during the previous one just a year ago).

* * *

Through a contact of Mum's I had obtained a summer job teaching for a month at a pop-up English language school just outside Brighton, where children from wealthy European families were offloaded while their parents enjoyed themselves back home, temporarily free of their offspring. Most of the staff were retired teachers, some of whom I suspect hadn't been very good at their job, and then there was student me.

One of the things I remember most from that time was the mid-morning coffee break, with a basket of mint Yo-Yo chocolate biscuits. Another was a Belgian girl with whom I went dancing one evening at the famous Regent in Brighton, and who later sent me as a surprise a parcel of Belgian cigarettes (everyone smoked in those days) on which I had to pay a lot of customs duty.

With the money I made from that not unpleasant summer job I arranged a pilgrimage across the north of Italy, beginning actually down south with my aunts in Naples, taking an overnight sleeper up to Milan (where I saw on the newspaper hoardings that the Russians had invaded Czechoslovakia overnight and crushed the Prague Spring) to stay with family in Monza, where I had a great-uncle and first cousins once removed.

From there I travelled eastwards across the north by train, stopping off at Mantua (with its amazing Monteverdi connections), Verona (which I didn't like, leaving as soon as I had seen Juliet's balcony, which was twee and the open-air opera, which repelled me), and Padua, where I admired frescoes by Giotto, explained to me by the girlfriend, one of Mum's students from her Italian class at the Brighton College of Art, I was with.

Next day we arrived in Venice and what a wonderful sight it was, emerging from the railway station onto the Grand Canal and seeing all that dreamlike glory. We stayed in an hostel near the Accademia (in separate dormitories, of course), and ate improvised meals every evening either dining al fresco on rolls, cheese and wine we had bought from a local salumeria, or sitting in a tiny fish restaurant eating mysterious creatures caught from the Adriatic.

The Teatro la Fenice was advertising two concerts from the New York Philharmonic Orchestra conducted by Leonard Bernstein, as part of their 1968 European tour. As students we obviously couldn't afford the price of concert tickets, so I wrote to Bernstein, c/o the Stage Door, explaining I was an impecunious music student with ambitions to become a conductor and would it be possible to sit in on his rehearsals?

No reply came and I realise now it was unrealistic to expect one, as there was no need for rehearsals of the same programme at every venue. But on the afternoon of the opening concert we were hanging around the stage door of La

Fenice when the orchestra arrived and I latched on to one of the players. It turned out he was one of the orchestra's percussionists (what a happy coincidence), Arnie Lang, and he said he would be glad of a guide around Venice, which we were able to offer. In return he said he would bring us to watch both concerts from backstage and arrange for me to meet Leonard Bernstein after the final one!

That evening we met Arnie at the stage door and we watched Leonard Bernstein arrive, a tiny be-cloaked man with a silver-topped cane, swishing into the backstage area. Arnie installed us in the wings and the concert began. Bernstein conducted Rossini's Thieving Magpie Overture, then handed over to his assistant for William Schuman's Third Symphony. After the interval Bernstein returned for Berlioz' Symphonie Fantastique (I can still see his manic facial expressions in the diabolic finale), in which, as the NYPO was short of one percussion player, the orchestra manager was roped in to play the bass drum. "I could have done that," I groaned to myself.

The second concert was Roy Harris' Third Symphony, which really gripped me and which is surely the greatest symphony ever to come out of America (it's the New World version of Sibelius Seven), and then Mahler's Fifth. This was the first time I'd heard either work and it was amazing when, one year later, Visconti's wonderful film Death in Venice, Dirk Bogarde the magisterial star, was released with that symphony's Adagietto as its incidental music.

At the end of the performance the applause was tumultuous. Every time Bernstein disappeared into the wings his assistant was there with a glass of scotch and a cigarette lit and Bernstein took a quick drag on them both before returning to the auditorium for yet another bow.

After the concert Arnie ushered me into the queue of Venetian socialites waiting to meet the great little man. Every jewel-dripping Contessa and escort gushed over the Mahler. "What's the matter with these f***ing people," Bernstein muttered to his assistant, "didn't they understand Roy Harris?"

And then it was my turn. "Thank you so much for the Roy Harris, Mr Bernstein. What a strong piece!" And the ice was broken.

We then spoke about the Mahler and Bernstein told me that he was convinced that had he been born 50 years earlier, he would have composed that symphony, and he explained how he and Mahler shared such temperamental and career affinities, and both were Jews.

I then asked him for advice, saying I had ambitions to become a conductor, and he immediately interrupted me. "You're Christopher Morley, aren't you!" He had read my letter and remembered me. I couldn't believe it.

"You could come over to New York and study with me," he continued, "and then go in for the Mitropoulos Conducting Competition."

I was almost speechless, knowing my parents would never allow me to accept such a cavalier invitation and abandon my degree course, but it had been made. I asked Bernstein to autograph the only scrap of paper I had with me, my room voucher from the hostel and it is now facing me as I write, framed together with an Elgar signed visiting-card.

Arnie took us for a very expensive coffee at Florian's in St Mark's Square and next morning we took him on a little tour of Venice. And I had become besotted with Leonard Bernstein, an emotional debt I was able to repay many years later.

*   *   *

My final year at University accordingly began with a sense of elation which never actually left me. Unlike my insecure return for the start of my second year I was now totally confident, at the top of the pecking-order and indeed I was so "in" as a king-pin of the Music Department that I was out the other side, some of the new intake of first-years feeling too timid to approach me.

Life was great, with lots of playing, accompanying, composing, conducting (not least Haydn's Midi Symphony for the lunchtime concert organised by Sally Groves, daughter of the conductor Sir Charles), and of course studying, John Joubert my inspiring and caring tutor.

As part of our graduation requirements, all students had to submit a 20,000 word dissertation. I chose as the subject of mine "The Style and Technique of Mozart's Mature Symphonies", and I really loved researching that and writing it up. Mozart had become so much a part of me (as he still is and always will be), and this was not work at all, but a labour of love.

Once my dissertation was finished I sent it off to Dad, who had a secretary who specialised in freelance typing-work. It came back three days later, immaculately presented and beautifully bound. After graduation I was told by Nigel Fortune, another amazing tutor who was surely the greatest polymath ever in music of all periods, that my Mozart was one of the three best dissertations they had ever seen since the War.

I sat the examinations, knowing that my harmony and counterpoint was not up to scratch, having been badly taught that at school and negligently at university (I remedied that later, teaching myself for a Trinity College of London diploma, which I cherish), and I emerged with my Lower Second-Class Honours Degree.

People who graduated with a 2/2 traditionally got round it by saying that it proved that we lower seconds had got the best out of university life, studying, yes, but also enjoying everything else that was on offer.

And that was certainly the truth with me, having got the most out of the whole university experience. Things are so different for university students nowadays, who seem to have no time to relish it all and paying thousands per annum to boot.

And now this is where we came in...

Chapter 5

ESCAPE FROM THE CHALK-FACE

Yes, I was in the wilderness as a freelance music critic, but I remained firmly established as a school music-teacher. I had begun as acting Head of Department in Walsall, moving on swiftly to become Head of Department at the serene St Paul's Grammar School in Edgbaston. I met Maureen, my wife, there and we put on musical shows together.

After the first night of one of them, Captain Noah and his Floating Zoo, half the school burnt down and we were terrified that the cause had been the candles stuck into gin bottles placed either side of the music-desk on my grand piano. In fact we were in the clear the fire had begun when paint-tins exploded as a result of the heater in the shed built by the decorators refurbishing some of the rooms.

We decided it was not a good idea to be working and living together 24 hours a day, so I moved to become Head of Department at the Earls High School in Halesowen, which until a year previously had been Halesowen Grammar School, founded in 1652.

I stayed there a fairly long time and really loved it all. We moved to a house just a couple of minutes' walk for me from the school, though a half-hour drive for Maureen to St Paul's, and I felt like James Hilton's Mr Chips. I made some amazing friendships with a bunch of my colleagues and we were really "all for one and one for all".

One of my closest friends was Dave Vass, who taught woodwork and technical drawing. We developed an addiction to backgammon and played before school, at breaktimes, at lunchtimes and after school. We had our backgammon chairs set under the window by the coffee-table in our little "B"-block staff room, and no-one dared sit in them.

Until one hapless student on teaching-practice appeared one day, entered the staffroom before anyone else at breaktime and was comfortably ensconced in our seats when Dave and I rolled in. You can imagine the kind, soft words we said to him in order to persuade him to vacate our thrones. He never sat in them again.

I remember one occasion when Maureen and I were at the Hippodrome for a Welsh National Opera performance. We emerged for the first interval and there in the foyer were Dave and his wife Chris, who happened to be in Birmingham (they lived in Kidderminster) and who worked out our logistics. It was a wonderful surprise encounter.

Another close friend was Keith Dodd, with whom I used to play chess. Keith was Head of History, but was deteriorating with multiple sclerosis. Though he was literally doddery, the kids were great with him, and gave him every support. They all loved him. I eventually wrote all his school reports for him, which he dictated, even my inscrutable handwriting being preferable to his incapacitated scrawl.

An ambitious Senior Master arrived, also a history teacher and therefore a member of Keith's department, and bullied Keith so much that Doddy walked out one afternoon and never came back. The rest of us never forgave that creature for that and he was dead in the water, so far as I was concerned, forevermore. The toad moved to a Headship in Cardiff and was later awarded a CBE for services to education. I wrote him a vitriolic letter... but slept on it and never posted it.

We had a staff football-team, in which I was rubbish (in fact my first-ever contribution was to handle the ball in our own penalty-area, resulting of course in a penalty-kick and goal). Our opponents were staff from other schools, the local police (which built up useful links) and the AA.

We also played cricket against similar opposition. I was a kind of Geoff Boycott batsman, blocking one end while the other bloke did the scoring, and I loved it. I also acquired a reputation as a very safe pair of hands whilst fielding (must be something about a musician's hand/eye co-ordination), and took some memorable catches on the boundary (in one staff v. school match a sixth-former was well set for a century until caught by me; he used to serve me in the Post Office years later, and never stopped grumbling that I'd spoilt his triumph). The only trouble was, though I was good at catching on the boundary, I had a terrible throw-back if any delivery out there didn't result in a wicket.

Wanting to be as immersed as much as possible in every game of cricket, I also became the team's official umpire, so when I wasn't batting, I was still at the crease (a kind of cricket critic, if you like – try saying that as a tongue-twister). After each game our official scorer and I would go deep into conference over a pint, like a couple of nerds.

And there was also the tennis. The school's tennis-courts were just a couple of minutes away from our house, so during summer evenings Maureen and I, my best friend (who still is) Richard and his wife Sue, and others would go down there to play. During summer holidays several of us staffroom mates would play there in the mornings, prior to a lunchtime pint at the Hare and Hounds.

One morning I was standing at the net in a game of doubles while my partner served. As the return came, ready for me to smash, my foot caught in the net and I fell to the ground, landing on my wrists. They seemed fine at the time, but a few days later, when I was conducting an amateur operatic society rehearsal of the Desert Song, I realised my wrists weren't working.

My wrists recovered, but that was the end of my tennis.

However, the conducting went on. Not only was I musical director of local amateur operatic societies (three together at one point), there was also the recently-formed Halesowen Symphony Orchestra which I was asked to take over after the grandiose ideas of its founder nearly brought about its collapse, but chiefly there were the shows at school.

Halesowen Grammar School had long had a tradition of presenting Gilbert and Sullivan productions, but I guessed, rightly or wrongly, that with the kind of intake the Earls High School now had, those would be difficult to continue. Gently, I persuaded the Play Committee into taking a different direction.

By an amazing stroke of fortune, John Proffitt joined our staff as a special needs teacher. He and I had been at Westlain together! We knew each other very well and had been involved in productions together at school. We decided to produce Oh, What a Lovely War! and the Play Committee had no choice but to acquiesce.

I got up at 6am every day to make orchestral parts from the vocal score, in order that the stick-in-the-muds had no grounds for objection as to the expense, we rehearsed every afternoon after school and the kids loved it all.

The lads in the Sixth-form really took the show on board, outraged to learn of the experiences of boys of their own age only 60 years previously (John and I had felt the same when studying the poems of Wilfred Owen for English 'A'-level just a few years earlier).

Traditionally, productions at the school had been introduced by the tolling of a gong, to summon and quieten the audience. John and I put a stop to that. I had seen too many productions at the Royal Shakespeare Theatre, beginning with all kinds of intriguing pre-curtain preludes, to put up with anything so peremptory. I think instead I tinkled some music-hall songs of the Great War period on the piano, before our little orchestra "bosted off", as they say in the Black Country.

We also insisted upon our names being printed in the programme, something which had never happened before (staff had always been involved anonymously).

We didn't require this out of vanity, but just to give the audience members a true picture of everyone who had been instrumental in bringing the production to life.

There was also a gag which ran for many years. John and I always used to joke with the kids that we were scrapping the current production and were going to do The Sound of Music instead. And in every show I used to slip in a quotation of that song during performance, on the piano if I was playing, or cued into an instrumental part if I was conducting. The kids used to love this "Spot the Quote".

John subsequently went on to star in some of our musicals. He sang the Defendant when I decided to put on Trial by Jury, just to show the old guard how difficult Gilbert and Sullivan now was, given the new status of the school (in fact it turned out to be a triumph, not least because Nobby Clarke, the producer and I cast Henry Penberthy, the Headmaster, as the Learned Judge, and Henry and the kids had a whale of a time working together). John also stepped in as Fagin in Oliver! at the very last minute, when the lad who had been cast in the role chickened out, and he later was Wild Bill Hickok in a very happy production of Calamity Jane.

Nobby Clarke was Head of English and he was a formidable, if inscrutable man. His voice-production was amazing, all built from the diaphragm, and he demonstrated to all our actors how to project their voice from the stage to the imaginary little old man sitting on the back row of the balcony. I have always maintained that voice-production should be taught to all trainee teachers, so many of whom go down with throat-strain within a few weeks of starting their teaching careers.

For all his bluster, Nobby was a very lonely man, and I guessed there had been a romantic disappointment long ago in his life. He had no real friends on the staff, though he was much respected as Head of English.

He and I worked marvellously together on shows, each admiring the other's expertise, and I particularly cherish the memory of our presiding in my music room during lunchtime auditions for whichever forthcoming musical.

I remember one occasion when we were planning to put on My Fair Lady (John Proffitt was a brilliant Dolittle), and we were still looking for our Eliza. Linda Webb, a quiet Fourth-Year girl who had never drawn any attention to herself in any way, stood demurely in the corner furthest away from my piano, and sang "Wouldn't it be loverly" and Nobby and I were knocked out by this girl's hidden talent. I was very moved and I doubt anybody at the Earls had ever seen Nobby also so moved.

Linda of course got the part and she was tremendous, developing from the little guttersnipe to the gracious lady, and the show was a triumph. During the performances the soloists often couldn't hear their next cue from the orchestra as the applause was so great after the end of each number. Thankfully they knew how to look to me to bring them in.

It was during the rehearsals for My Fair Lady that it became my privilege to get to know Nobby really well. One night at the end of rehearsal I asked him if he'd like to go for a drink and we drove over to the Queen's Head, which in those days was a local par excellence (and where I used to treat myself to a pint and a cheese-and-tomato cob after an evening's reviewing, and on Christmas Eve I would play carols on the battered old grand piano in the corner under the stairs – and envy the chap who was Father Christmas, with all the pretty girls sitting on his knee).

During that conversation over three pints I learned so much about Nobby, about his childhood, his schooling, the places where he'd worked – and his crush on Audrey Hepburn! Perhaps his work on our own My Fair Lady was a homage to her.

A few years later we put on Oliver! for a second time and the final night of the run brought about an amazing chain of events which you really couldn't make up.

Welsh National Opera were performing Die Walkure, my favourite opera out of Wagner's Ring tetralogy, and I had press tickets to go and see it at Birmingham Hippodrome. But I had a show to conduct at school! How to get round it?

The conductor for Walkure was the legendary Reginald Goodall, he who had been the powerhouse behind the unforgettable Mastersingers we had all gone down to see from university at Sadler's Wells in 1968, and he was very infirm. I had this fantasy in my head. What if I were sitting in the auditorium and the call came out, Mr Goodall is unwell, is there a conductor in the house? What would I do? Jump onto the podium and take over and let down all the kids at school? No, I could never allow myself to do that.

This is how the logistics of the evening worked. I donned my dinner-suit ready for conducting the final night of Oliver! and we drove to the Hippodrome, in time for the opera's very early start. In those days I always used to park on the forecourt of a petrol station just up the side from the theatre.

We took our seats and enjoyed Act One, then I passed Maureen into the care of Ghita Ogg, Head of Modern Languages at St Paul's (who as a young Czech girl had escaped from the Nazis across Europe into neutral Portugal), who entertained her to a picnic supper with her friends.

I, meanwhile, was bombing back to Halesowen, ready for the final performance of Oliver! It went very well, despite the fact that in my mind I was following the unfolding of Walkure at the Hippodrome – so "Food, Glorious Food" became interwoven with The Ride of the Valkyries.

The show ended, I congratulated the cast briefly (perhaps too briefly, as they had bought me a lovely tie as a last-night present), and hurtled back into Birmingham. I was able to park in the little petrol station again, made my imperious way back into the Hippodrome auditorium, in time to stand at the back for the conclusion of Die Walkure, Wotan's Farewell, which is one of the most emotional scenes in all opera.

At the end of the performance I strode down the aisle to our seats near the front of the stalls, with everyone looking at this dinner-suited person making his way forward, wondering if he were the conductor, entering for his curtain-call. My seat next to Maureen had been taken, as she had offered it to a student standing at the back, so I continued down to the edge of the orchestra pit, where I saw the amazing sight of all the players standing in homage while a couple of burly attendants raised the infirm Reginald Goodall by his elbows, carrying him through the pit and up onto the stage, where he received tumultuous applause.

Maureen's student thanked me profusely for the use of my seat, and she and I drove back home to Halesowen. I changed out of my conducting gear, and then went on to the after-Oliver party at the home of the young man who had played Fagin. At last I could relax after an astonishing evening.

*   *   *

My schoolteaching career was coming to an end. I loved being with the kids, I loved the classroom experience, I loved the mates I had bonded with, but I didn't like the way I saw the system was going.

I saw an advertisement that a music shop, Cottage Music Moseley, was up for sale and Maureen and I went to look it over. It was charming, up a little entry and tucked under St Mary's Church, whose property it actually was. John Joubert, who lived nearby, described it as a "little cathedral close". Mike Perrier, organist at the church, was the founder and proprietor, but was anxious to get out (that should have rung a warning bell).

I was taken with the idea of becoming an avuncular music-shopkeeper and took it on, despite an accountant warning me against it. At the end of the Easter term in 1987 there was the usual staff-meeting at the Earls, and there were various farewells to departing members of staff. Mine came at the end and I could tell the tributes to me and my years of service were sticking in the headmistress's craw. I was presented with a barometer and bottle of whisky, and that was that.

Next morning I became a fulltime shopkeeper and what an eye-opener that experience proved to be. I came into contact with so many lovely customers, but also with a few nasty types and several time-wasters, so I learnt a lot about human nature and I'm afraid that hardened me a little in certain respects.

Simon Rattle bought an emergency baton from me, Peter Donohoe ordered Messiaen scores from me, John Joubert snaffled all 15 Shostakovich String Quartet scores I'd just acquired as the result of a huge estate disposal, and many CBSO players used to pop in for things. There were also lots of lovely local regulars who used to shop at Cottage Music.

All of this was rose-tinted and idyllic, but then there came the most amazing turning-point in my life.

*   *   *

The Birmingham Post was about to relieve its current Chief Music Critic of his duties, as he was becoming risibly accident-prone. He had recently written a review of Shostakovich's Fifth Symphony when he had actually been hearing a performance of Prokofiev's Fifth Symphony; these Soviet symphonies are all the bloody same, was his response when challenged at the paper next morning.

Terry Grimley, Arts Editor of the Birmingham Post, and who lived in Moseley, came into Cottage Music late one afternoon and asked me if I fancied a pint and a chat. I closed up the shop and we went to the Bull's Head, just a few steps down the road.

He explained that the Post was looking for a new Chief Music Critic and he needed to pick my brains. What did I think of so-and-so? Or so-and-so? And how about the person who was pushing himself as chief candidate? "No, not him," I replied. "He knows nothing earlier than 1700, and can't cope with contemporary music." In fact this gentleman later acquired much egg on his face when giving a pre-concert talk in Bromsgrove, deriding the Piano Quintet of Alfred Schnittke which was about to be played. At the end of the performance many of the audience were moved to tears and the reputation of this so-called authority was in tatters.

A few days later Terry was in touch again, offering me the post of Chief Music Critic of the Birmingham Post! Of course I accepted like a shot, honoured to be following in the footsteps of such as Ernest Newman (who had built such a name for himself despite being in my opinion something of a fraud), Eric Blom (a hero) and John Waterhouse.

A contract was speedily drawn up, I was introduced to the Editor and to the Features Editor, Jonathan Daumler-Ford, a lovely man with an inexplicable love of Donizetti operas, as well as being heavily into rock music. He was such a sad loss when stomach cancer claimed him a few years later, and he and I were so pleased to see each other when I visited him on his death-bed at the Queen Elizabeth Hospital. Dear Jonathan.

The official date of my appointment was April 1 1988 (yes, how appropriate), but in fact I actually took up my duties before then, when Terry asked me to write a feature about the Mozart Requiem which was about to be performed by a local choral society. Mozart and his Requiem could not have been a better shoe-in for what has been at the time of writing nearly a third of a century in a post which has brought me so much joy, so many friendships, and so much professional acceptance around the world.

As I wrote earlier, my first review wearing my new hat was actually a TV relay of the CBSO in the United States. Someone wrote to the newspaper complaining about my comments about Simon Rattle's facial expressions, but let us not forget, I was reviewing this as a television broadcast as well as a concert. Then came the unforgettable Milan experience.

After which I came down to earth with a bump, reviewing a concert in a Bromsgrove High school whose auditorium smelt of urine, but also becoming a presence in the Birmingham Post's traditional seats in the Lower Gallery at Birmingham Town Hall for CBSO concerts.

Simon Rattle was now eight years into his tenure as Principal Conductor and he was obtaining amazing results from his willing orchestra, and together we all built a rewarding collaboration, devoted to the success of the orchestra and therefore to music-making itself.

In those heady days the CBSO could afford to invite me to go on tour with them, and there were so many tours I shared: Germany, France, Finland, Estonia, Romania, Austria, and the players – and conductors – treated me not with suspicion as an hostile critic (I have never been that), but as a supportive friend.

On one occasion we were about to fly from Birmingham International Airport to Romania, about a week after the 9/11 atrocity in New York, and the security was understandably very tight. I had a tiny pair of folding scissors in my wash-bag, given to me by my mother nearly 30 years earlier, and she had now passed on. And they were confiscated.

I explained all this to the security guard, saying how much they meant to me in terms of sentimental value and then something extraordinary happened, which couldn't happen now in these security-fraught days. He took my name and address and when I got back from the trip, there, waiting for me at home was a little package containing Mum's scissors! I wanted to write about it in the paper, but realised it would cause a bit of a furore, with everyone expecting such personalised treatment. I still use those scissors almost every day, trimming my moustache (but without the vanity, I hope, of Hercule Poirot).

Another time the CBSO and I were in Paris, where Simon was conducting Brahms' Fourth Symphony and Stravinsky's Rite of Spring (what a strange programme) at the historic Salle Pleyel. Early in the evening it was pouring with rain and I was teetering on the pavement, trying to cross the road through the traffic. "Don't jump, Chris!" said this Paddington Bear-clad figure who had come up beside me. It was Simon.

And then there was the occasion of the famous argument between Simon and me in Frankfurt. He was conducting the CBSO in Mahler's Sixth Symphony (in my opinion the greatest symphony of the 20th century), in which there is a perennial controversy over the order of the middle movements, which is entirely Mahler's fault. His original plan was to have the scherzo as the second movement, followed by the slow movement, but for some reason after the premiere decided to reverse the order.

Never mind that such minor conductors as Herbert von Karajan, Leonard Bernstein and Bernard Haitink kept to the original order of movements, many, including Simon Rattle, decided to go with Mahler's revision (ignoring the fact that just before his death he decided to rescind and go back to his original layout).

There was a dinner for the great and good (and me) after this Frankfurt concert, and the conversation was buzzing in little groups, but it all gradually died down as everyone tuned in to the argument Simon and I were having about the Mahler movement-order.

"Simon, you need to postpone the solace of the slow movement until after the scherzo, which continues the pounding assault of the first movement," I said. "Then comes the repose until the finale bludgeons us into oblivion."

Simon wouldn't have it and went on about Mahler's own revisions, and seemed oblivious when I pointed out that at the end of his life Mahler revised back. It was all very amicable and we remain on very good terms to this day. He and I had a lovely exchange of emails from his car as he was being driven back to London after a Berg/Beethoven concert in Symphony Hall with the London Symphony Orchestra a few months ago.

Chapter 6

BIRMINGHAM POST CHIEF MUSIC CRITIC

That LSO concert was the latest in the many triumphant returns Simon Rattle has made to the world-class concert hall which he had brought into existence, and the auditorium was as packed on this occasion as it had been on that heady night when the Hall opened, on April 15 1991.

It had been obvious for years, going back in fact to Adrian Boult's first tenure with the then City of Birmingham Orchestra, that Birmingham Town Hall, for all its wonderful atmosphere and awesome history (Mendelssohn looking down on us all from his organ-loft), was no longer fit for the CBSO's purpose. The stage was cramped, backstage facilities were minimal, and the acoustic could not do justice to the wonderful sounds Rattle was drawing from his orchestra.

Thanks to some adroit negotiating led by Tom Caulcott (Birmingham City Council's Chief Executive – incidentally, he looked so much like Wagner and his wife Jayne Alsopp so much like Cosima!) funding was secured from the European Union to build an International Convention Centre in a derelict canalside area just off rundown Broad Street, one of the gateways into Birmingham city centre.

This ICC was to house many conference rooms of various sizes, including a mysterious Hall 2, which was to have seating for 2200 people. Surreptitiously Hall 2 was to morph into a concert hall, brilliantly christened "Symphony Hall" by CBSO Chief Executive Officer Edward Smith, and its design was meticulously planned.

Ove Arup were the architects, but crucially the world's greatest acoustician, Russell Johnston of New York-based Artec, was brought in to design the auditorium itself, its shape, its layout, and its ability to be flexible in response to the requirements of every kind of performance on offer.

The results were spectacular: a canopy above the stage which could be raised or lowered in order to reflect the sound of anything from a huge symphony orchestra to an intimate chamber ensemble; panels aloft on the top tier which could be utilised for the same purposes; and acoustic chambers on every level, whose doors could be opened wide to create a cathedral sound.

Russell was a lovely man. He was aware of his skills (I think false modesty is a waste of everyone's time – you may have gathered that!), but also quite humble. A few years after the triumphant opening of Symphony Hall I visited him in his studio in Manhattan and he proudly showed me little shoe-box models of the 50-odd concert halls he had designed around the world.

To describe the opening of Symphony Hall as an amazing success would be an understatement. Rattle and the CBSO gave two mini-concerts and in my capacity I was present at both (and the three receptions before, between and after them).

They began with Stravinsky's complete score for his Firebird ballet, and right from the very first bars I could tell that Birmingham now had a concert hall worthy of its world-class orchestra and conductor. You could hear, as never before, the articulation of the double-basses, some of them pizzicato, some of them arco, underpinned by an ominous bass-drum roll.

You could also hear, though, every rustle from the audience, every cough, every pin drop. But the players could hear each other as never before, which for some was at first quite disconcerting, but which truly enhanced the rehearsal and performance experience.

The second mini-concert was a performance of the complete score of Ravel's Daphnis and Chloe, which of course also involved the CBSO Chorus. We were in different seats for this, so I had already had two aural perspectives of the hall, but not yet from the seats which have remained permanently mine for CBSO concerts to this day, and which I selected at a pre-hearing before Symphony Hall officially opened.

This was a late-running evening and I had to tiptoe out of the auditorium while the concert was continuing in order to phone in my review. A press room had been arranged on the artists' corridor with phones and note-pads on the tables, but it seemed I was the only one dictating an overnight review. Seeing it in print next morning, accompanied by a brilliant cartoon picking up my comment about the acoustic from the Birmingham Post's late-night, topical cartoonist Gemini (Bert Hackett), gave me a great sense of achievement.

I made my way back into the auditorium, stifling any objections from the steward on the door with my famous schoolmaster's and conductor's glare (no wonder the kids used to call me Mr Death and performers at the operatic society would take bets as to who was going to get the glare tonight), and caught the end of the Ravel and the tumultuous applause.

And then more champagne.

Next day I had a scoop for the Birmingham Post. Simon Rattle was going to ring me at teatime to give me, and me alone, his reaction to the hall after this opening evening. He was ecstatic and so grateful to the City fathers who had brought Symphony Hall into the world. This was front-page news the following morning.

Five years later Manchester opened its Bridgewater Hall and I was invited to the inaugural concert there. I had already been to investigate the site during the building process (and was jealous that there was already an organ, which Symphony Hall didn't have), at the end of which visit I was taken for lunch by the Press Officer, who had the longest name on a credit card I have ever seen (she was of Dutch descent).

They put us up in the Midland Hotel, just across the square from the Hall itself (from which I popped down to the Granada Studios to interview the American composer John Adams), and then while Maureen and I were changing in our comfortable room we had the bizarre experience of watching a broadcast on the local television station, live from the Hall, just a few yards from us, anticipating the evening which was coming up.

It seemed that half the cast of Coronation Street (one of whom refused to stand for the National Anthem) were in the comfortable auditorium, along with the great footballer Denis Law, who had turned down a trip to Turin where a match between two of his clubs, Juventus and Manchester City, was being played that evening.

At the end of the concert from the Halle Orchestra and Chorus, Kent Nagano conducting Elgar's Enigma Variations, and Walton's Belshazzar's Feast (Thomas Allen the baritone soloist), I phoned in my review and was thrilled to be able to say, hand-on-heart, that the acoustic couldn't quite match up to Symphony Hall's (the middle register – i.e. viola range – was lacking).

My review appeared in the Birmingham Post the very next morning and I was very proud of myself. I had been the first critic in the world to publish immediate reviews of both Birmingham's Symphony Hall and Manchester's Bridgewater Hall (beating in the latter instance even my good friend Robert Beale of the Manchester Evening News).

But I have moved forward several years, so let's get back to Symphony Hall. The official opening was set for June 12 1991 and the Queen came to unveil the plaque, attend the CBSO's rehearsal for that evening's concert, and to be photographed with Simon Rattle and some of the players and staff.

But she and Prince Philip decided to skip the concert itself and went back to put their feet up in Buckingham Palace, leaving Princess Anne to sit through Mahler's Resurrection Symphony, the signature work throughout Simon Rattle's career.

Anne was there chairing a conference of the International Olympic Committee and complimentary tickets for that evening's concert had been issued to all the delegates. Unfortunately hardly any of them bothered to attend, so there was the scandal of rows of empty seats shown to the world when BBC2 broadcast the event live. That was not a good advertisement for Birmingham and its great new concert hall.

But one person who was prominently seen throughout that broadcast was Maureen! The television camera homing in directly onto Simon Rattle also focussed past his left shoulder into the auditorium and onto a blonde woman wearing a pale green dress sitting in the stalls – Maureen.

The jungle drums on the family phone lines went red-hot (I was impressed they were even watching such a cultural programme) and everyone clicked on their video-recorders. But the seat next to Maureen seemed to be empty! How was that?

The reason was that the chief music critic of the Birmingham Post continually had his head down, out of camera sight, scribbling his notes, ready to phone in his review. Which he did, immediately the concert was over.

We had been invited to supper in Hall One at the ICC, but the queues looked immense, so we decided not to bother, driving instead back home, where I presented myself at the Halesowen chippie in my dinner-suit for fish and chips which made a delicious end to the evening.

During those early years at Symphony Hall I built a wonderful relationship with the staff, from the backstage management to the stewards, who all grew to recognise me and were always welcoming.

Above all was the friendship I forged with Andrew Jowett, Director of Symphony Hall (and later too, of Birmingham Town Hall), a wonderful, vibrant, generous man who loved where he was at and never failed to show it. He was always mine host in the Green Room (now called the Director's Lounge), and his hospitality was the stuff of legends.

Andrew has now retired from THSH (Town Hall Symphony Hall – they had to be careful about the letter-order of that acronym, in case it could be carelessly misread), and I miss his presence, though we remain very good friends. In a way we built the reputation of Symphony Hall together.

Simon Rattle of course had his own designated dressing-room on the artists' corridor and it had the only bath in the whole of the International Convention Centre complex. Not only had Simon brought about the very existence of Symphony Hall, he had insisted upon having a bath installed in which to soak away post-concert strains.

He certainly did make that room his own, with drawings from his two young sons displayed on the walls, and a framed portrait of his great conducting hero, Wilhelm Furtwangler. Over the years I interviewed not only him in that room, but many visiting conductors, such as Pierre Boulez, Valery Gergiev, Mark Elder (who, discussing Delius with me, said "didn't that composer have balls, Chris!"), and lovely John Wilson, with whom I developed a very warm relationship (there are in fact two other important John Wilsons in the arts world, one of them the Manchester-based pianist whom every great pianist from that part of the country – Peter Donohoe, Martin Roscoe among them – refers to as "God", the other the BBC Radio 4 broadcaster on arts topics).

I knew that conductor John, a great champion of British light music, had been presented with Eric Coates' wristwatch by that wonderful composer's son. At the end of a public interview with John, onstage in Symphony Hall before a CBSO concert, I casually asked him "what's the time, John?", he looked at his watch and that was the opportunity for one more anecdote.

On another occasion, I was at the Royal Albert Hall for a CBSO Prom, and an anonymous figure in shades came up and greeted me. It was John! He was there in the audience to support this orchestra he loved so much. I told him I'd been invited to an interval reception and would he like to join me? I gave him the details of where it would be.

Unfortunately I gave him details of the wrong reception, so he ended up gate-crashing one while I was at the proper one. He didn't bear a grudge, though. Which became obvious when he gave my dear friend Angela Daniels one of her most abiding memories. Angela and I had shared a wonderful working relationship for many years in the local operatic society, she as a brilliant choreographer as well as soloist, me as music director, and I had been thrilled to be asked to be Best Man at her wedding with Tony.

John was conducting an MGM film musicals concert with the CBSO and Maureen was unable to accompany me. I asked Angela and Tony to fight among themselves to see who would like to fill my vacant spare seat and Angela won.

Most performers don't like being disturbed during concert intervals, but John never minded my visiting his dressing-room (I remember once taking my Dad in there, and John was so courteous and kind to him). On this occasion I took

Angela into the Director's Lounge for a drink and then along the corridor to John's dressing-room.

I knocked on the door, heard the "Come in" (how I hate the summons "Come" which is so often used in mediocre television dramas), and we entered the sanctum. John was on the sofa, drinking a glass of water, and greeted me warmly.

I introduced Angela, who always liked to have an appropriate question prepared and she asked John, "you conduct so much dance music so well, are you a dancer yourself?" At which John grabbed hold of her and quickstepped her around the dressing-room!

Angela was all of a flutter after that.

But let's get back to Symphony Hall and the crucial difference it made not only to concert-life in Birmingham but also in the country as a whole.

Thanks to Symphony Hall we were now able to hear the first professional performance in Birmingham of Mahler's Eighth Symphony, the alleged "Symphony of a Thousand" (only about half that, actually, even at the Mahler-conducted premiere in Munich on September 11 1910), Mark Elder conducting CBSO forces. We later heard it here from the National Youth Orchestra of Great Britain, and an amazing amateur performance from the Birmingham Philharmonic Orchestra, conducted by the wonderful but disgracefully under-rated Michael Lloyd.

We also had the Birmingham premiere of Schoenberg's Gurrelieder, a work which might have been composed for the power and responsiveness of the CBSO under Simon Rattle, with so many demands in terms of instrumentation (even chains in the percussion section, would you believe) and spacing of forces. Symphony Hall can do all that, with all its galleries, balconies, levels and acoustic chambers, and the result was mind-blowing.

I had bought myself a miniature score of the piece from Cottage Music, but had problems following it, as I had an eye-complaint at the time which was eventually solved through brilliant surgery, but that didn't mar my memory of an epic evening from the CBSO and Rattle. Among the many soloists was Philip Langridge, a tenor I admired so much, and with whom I was to have a wonderful post-show conversation at the reception after a CBSO performance of Janacek's opera Jenufa at the Châtelet in Paris.

"I've seen you many times in the pews," he said. I seem to remember quaffing a fair amount of Pernod during that trip, a drink I must get to grips with again.

I have already referred to my chagrin that Manchester's Bridgewater Hall already had an organ installed, right at the beginning of its existence. All we had at Symphony Hall was the rather splendid casing, but no actual instrument. It was to be all of ten years after the Hall's opening before the magnificent Klais organ was built, but it was an event worth waiting for, with a whole weekend of celebrations featuring the CBSO, principal conductor Sakari Oramo, and of course Thomas Trotter, the lovely man who was (and still is) the City Organist.

I remember Tommy playing at a fund-raising event on temporary instruments for the building of the organ, sharing an evening with the flamboyant American organist Carlo Curley (who liked to describe himself as "the Pavarotti of the organ" – well, yes, they were similarly built). The final item was a transcription of Wagner's Ride of the Valkyries, for which Tommy and Carlo both wore horned helmets. I have never seen mild, modest Tommy Trotter look so embarrassed.

The largest organ pipes had to be delivered by narrowboat, along the canal which flanked Symphony Hall. That was quite an occasion, but I was unable to be present, as I was down somewhere near the Hippodrome (was it the Albany Hotel?) for a press conference with the great tenor Jose Carreras, who was due to perform in Birmingham the next night.

It was a pleasant press conference, during which I congratulated Carreras on behalf of my Neapolitan mother, who thought he sang the songs of her native city better than Pavarotti, Carreras' great friend and rival (incidentally, both have sung in Birmingham; the only one of the famous Three Tenors not to have done so is Placido Domingo, though he did once appear on the stage of Symphony Hall to receive an award).

At the end, as I was making my farewells, Carreras asked me to give his best wishes to my mother! I then had to rush to the offices of the Birmingham Post and write up the feature, for which they were holding the presses, the senior editorial staff all waiting deferentially.

Rather than me blowing my own trumpet, back to the Symphony Hall organ, which was a magnificent instrument with two consoles, one proudly, spectacularly aloft at the top of the choir-stalls, the other a portable one which could be nestled onstage amid the orchestra. People had been asked to sponsor pipes; Dad, 200 miles away in Eastbourne, sponsored two, one for himself, the other in memory of Mum (and he came up for that heady inaugural weekend), and I sponsored one as well.

Another sponsorship I was involved in was when the CBSO opened its much-needed centre as an administrative and rehearsal home in Berkley Street, just a few minutes' walk away from Symphony Hall, and whose acoustic was designed to replicate that of what had become a world-renowned auditorium.

I sent in a small financial contribution, but also wrote an article for the Birmingham Post which was included in the time-capsule buried under the floor of the main hall, addressed to the reader of the future. Also included in the capsule was a tiny cross of nails made by Maggie Cotton's father out of the debris of Coventry Cathedral, bombed during World War II. Maggie had long been a much-loved percussionist in the CBSO, and is now one of my valued team reviewing for the Birmingham Post.

My position with the newspaper brought me into contact with so many top names in the world of music and the number of disappointing interviewees out of hundreds could be counted on the fingers of one hand. Virtually all of them were charming, responsive and appreciative of the care with which I had prepared the questions for our interviews. Many were carried out over the phone, in later years the majority were via email, but here are just a few of the face-to-face ones which were particularly memorable.

I arranged to meet the percussionist Evelyn Glennie at the Midlands Arts Centre in Cannon Hill Park one Friday afternoon and we sat on the grass while I interviewed her. Interestingly, she kept referring to herself in the third person, as though this great musician were a separate entity. At the end of the interview I took her back to Cottage Music, where her manager was coming to collect her, but we were still able to continue our conversation as we drove there in my car, Evelyn (who of course is profoundly deaf) lip-reading everything from the passenger-seat beside me.

Some years later I interviewed her again, one Sunday morning at an hotel in Birmingham. Her then partner and roadie, Greg Malcangi was with her. I discovered that he, like me, was half-Neapolitan, and we started to converse in that complex dialect – and Evelyn was able to keep up with us, lip-reading our Neapolitan from a sideways angle!

I was (and remain) a great fan of the Russian conductor Yuri Temirkanov, whose debut concert with the CBSO so long ago had been characterised by his giving orchestral entries with his head, like the great centre-forward Jeff Astle scoring a goal for West Bromwich Albion. He was conducting the Royal Philharmonic Orchestra at the Royal Concert Hall in Nottingham, and I drove over to interview him. During the journey I played the cassette of him conducting Rachmaninov's gorgeous Second Symphony.

We did the interview, assisted by a formidable Russian interpreter. She kept a firm eye on him, and had the vodka bottle firmly locked away pre-concert! At the end of our interesting conversation, during which we talked, among other things, about the cuts conductors used to make in certain works – the Rachmaninov,

Tchaikovsky's Manfred Symphony – in those days, I produced my cassette of the Rachmaninov and asked him to sign it.

We continued talking while he scribbled on the inside of the cover. And eventually he returned it to me. There was no signature, but a caricature of himself with a cigarette drooping from his lower lip, looking totally dissolute! I still treasure that cassette and its cover.

Perhaps one of the most unexpected interviews was my conference call with Neil Sedaka, arranged by his agent in London so that I wouldn't have to pay the expense of a lengthy conversation between Halesowen and Manhattan. Sedaka would shortly be coming to perform at Symphony Hall and I knew he had been trained up to the highest echelons of classical pianism, and this would make a great feature.

His songs Happy Birthday, Sweet Sixteen and Breaking up is hard to do had been the signature-tunes of my teens, so it was good to thank him for those, but then he was so thrilled to talk about his classical background, and the fact that Artur Rubinstein had awarded him first prize in an important competition. And, also, that the International Tchaikovsky Piano Competition in Moscow had rejected him as a participant on the grounds that he was a commercial pop singer in a capitalist country.

Then there was the great American baritone Thomas Hampson. He was coming to Birmingham to perform and record Mahler's Das Lied von der Erde with the CBSO and Simon Rattle, and I went down to London to interview him at his hotel, the Savoy.

I sat in the foyer waiting for him to turn up for the appointment, but no Thomas Hampson. Eventually the phone rang at Reception and I was called over to take the call. It was from him. He was Christmas shopping with his wife in Oxford Street and had totally forgotten our arrangement! Unfortunately my return train had been booked and I couldn't hang around any longer.

His apologies were profuse and he rang me at home the next morning in order to carry out the interview. Then he said, "look, why don't we meet for a drink when I come up to Birmingham?" and that is what we did.

I met him at the Hyatt Hotel, where he was staying, but he didn't like the stiff atmosphere of the bar there, so we walked the hundred yards down Bridge Street to the James Brindley pub on Gas Street basin. As we entered the place the air was thick with cigarette smoke, and I recoiled, fearful that Hampson would be anxious about his throat.

"F**k that," he exclaimed, "Come on, I want some of your excellent bitter!" And we had an engrossing, wide-ranging conversation over three pints.

Totally different was my interface with Karlheinz Stockhausen, one of the most significant and influential composers of the 20th century, and a figure of whom many musicians and writers felt themselves in awe. I had first encountered his music during my undergraduate years, listening to concerts at the Barber Institute presenting some of his electronic music and some of his "moment-form" piano works (I was later to enjoy teaching the ideas behind this brilliant new structural invention to the students in my Music Since World War II class at Birmingham Conservatoire).

Early on in my career as a critic I reviewed his Stimmung, a work for six unaccompanied voices performed in the virtual dark by Songcircle, and I described it as one of the sexiest pieces of music I knew. Later there was to be an awesome performance of Stockhausen's Gruppen from the CBSO in Hall One of the ICC (requiring three orchestras spatially separated it needed that vast area), conducted by Simon Rattle, his mentor John Carewe and his protege Daniel Harding (whose first-ever concert as a professional conductor I had reviewed at Warwick Arts Centre). There were two performances during that memorable evening, and we were encouraged to sit in different parts of the hall in order to gain varying aural perspectives.

But most spectacular of all, and memorable for me, was the visit Stockhausen made to Birmingham to preside over a performance of his Sternklang, "Park Music". This is an absolutely fascinating piece which can only be performed as sunset approaches, in the open air by five groups of musicians arranged around a park, with "messengers" running between the groups relaying the next musical idea, and periodically running to a central hub where a gong signals key moments. Its climax comes as the moon rises and everything subsides as this lengthy offering comes to an end.

Sternklang was to be presented in the ideal location of Cannon Hill Park in leafy, bird-singing Edgbaston, and Stockhausen came over from his German base to supervise rehearsals from the five different local music groups (Birmingham Contemporary Music Group, Birmingham Conservatoire and the University of Birmingham among them). He had based himself in the Grand Hotel in Colmore Row and I was going there to interview him – apparently the only critic who dared! – late on Saturday afternoon.

So, I shut up Cottage Music for the weekend, and went over to the car park, only to find a flat tyre on my car! I changed the wheel (you could do that in those days, before those daft little temporary spares had been invented), and drove into Birmingham for my appointment with the great man.

Unfortunately my hands were filthy after changing the wheel, and I hadn't had the chance to wash them, so there was no handshake between us. Stockhausen had his habitual entourage of two ladies draped around his chair while he and I conversed in what was a lovely interview.

The weather was filthy too, and non-stop rain was forecast right up to the performance on the Tuesday, four days later. Stockhausen was very worried about it. "Don't worry," I reassured him, "it will all have cleared up by Tuesday evening."

Tuesday evening came, and indeed the rain had gone, leaving everything delightfully fresh and summery. Cannon Hill Park was packed, and there was a considerable venom of critics (the composer John Woolrich's collective noun, which he gave me at Aldeburgh many, many years later) assembled.

Everyone was exploring the park, listening to the performance from different perspectives and it was an amazing experience. Suddenly I encountered the white-suited Stockhausen and we at last shook hands. "Thank you for making the weather improve for me," he smiled.

The moon came up, the performance ended and we all went home, somewhat stunned by what we had shared in. I wrote my review and thought that was that.

But a few days later a package from Germany arrived at my house. As I unwrapped it, a double-CD of Sternklang emerged. And on the central spine was signed in white marker, "for Christopher Morley – Stockhausen 17.7.92".

Chapter 7

COTTAGE MUSIC CLOSES ITS DOORS

My elevation at the Birmingham Post could never have come about had I still been a full-time schoolteacher, but now I had the freedom to be flexible with my time-keeping, interviewing people during the day, attending press conferences, and even entertaining interviewees in Cottage Music itself.

I also did a bit of tuition in the shop, giving private theory lessons. One of my students was the daughter of a couple of local freelance musicians, her mother a flautist, her father a cellist and she needed coaching in Grade Five theory. She went on to become very successful in the world of theatrical production and eventually became the wife of Ronnie Wood, guitarist with the Rolling Stones.

There was always a bottle of wine in my little kitchenette from which I would treat my favoured customers (and of course myself in solitary lunches), which made me feel that I was being a shopkeeper out of a pre-war novel.

But the trouble with all these activities, which I loved doing, was that I was working what I liked to call "Gentleman's hours" in the shop, closing when I needed to, going out for extended lunches (including a monthly one in the Greek restaurant over the road with a lovely chap called Michael Green, who later became part of the administration at Birmingham Hippodrome), and often closing the shop early in order to get back home before the rush hour and then drive out again for a concert in Birmingham that night.

The shop telephone was also a newspaper phone, whether for doing an interview or for making an appointment for one, and during those calls it was of course out of action for customers wishing to place an order.

I was also doing a bit of supply teaching to boost my struggling income and on those occasions Maureen would drive over to Moseley to mind the shop.

And one Saturday she came to keep the shop all day while I took time off to watch the Test Match, just down the road in Edgbaston, with my best friend Richard and Simon, his son and my godson.

Towards the end of the afternoon I needed to use the facilities, when I got back to my seat Richard said they'd been calling for me on the Tannoy and I needed to go to the Press Box.

I thought my Neville Cardus moment had come! Cardus had been not only a great music critic on the Manchester Guardian, he also covered cricket matches for that respected newspaper, including Test Matches in Australia. Had the cricket correspondent of the Birmingham Post been taken ill, and did they want me to take over?

I made my excited way around the ground and entered the Press Box, where there were rows of journalists sitting at typewriters, adding to their copy after every delivery. But no, I hadn't been called there. You'd better try the Secretary's office, they said.

And there I trotted, to hear that Maureen had rung the ground to say she couldn't leave the shop as she'd returned to the car to discover she'd flattened the battery, having left the lights on all day. We were supposed to be going to a CBSO performance of Mendelssohn's Elijah that evening, conducted by the great German-Spanish conductor Rafael Fruhbeck de Burgos in the Town Hall where Mendelssohn had premiered the work in 1846, the concert to be televised live on BBC2.

But there was no way Maureen and I could get home and back in time for that concert, so instead we stayed in the shop, munching fish and chips, and then caught a taxi to the Town Hall. It was only at the end of the evening, after a wonderful performance, that, returning to the shop, we were able at last to call out the AA to bring life back to the battery and we could go home.

All these escapades were detrimental to the successful running of Cottage Music as a business and I realised I was losing a lot of money. During the summer of 1993 I agonised over what could be done and then, at last, one night when I was in Naples with Dad, visiting my aunt, his sister-in-law, who was going down with Alzheimer's, I came to the decision to shut the shop down and see what would come along.

That was such a liberating moment and I immediately felt much better. I spent that autumn gradually running down the stock as best I could, holding a clearance sale, until at last on Christmas Eve I locked up for the last time, and walked down through my little cathedral close as a Dickensian fog clustered around the tower of St Mary's Church above, carefully carrying Beethoven, my loyal goldfish who had kept me such great company, safely in his tank.

Cottage Music was no more.

*   *   *

Running this little business so ineptly cost me a lot of money, but fortunately I did have other trickling sources of income, not least the work at the Birmingham Post.

I had also been doing some supply teaching, chiefly to exam groups, in various local schools. A special memory from one of them, in a very deprived part of the Black Country, was when a group of third-year girls (nowadays Year 9) came up to me and asked if we could have a choir, sir. So, every lunchtime that I was there (only once a week, I think), they presented themselves in the music room and we worked on a pop song they were very keen on "Eternal Flame", which I turned into a two-part choral arrangement. It was a beautiful experience, and every time that song comes onto the radio now I feel quite emotional.

I also began working for the OCR examinations syndicate, examining 'A'-level Music Performance. This was a really enjoyable activity every spring, travelling the country to sit in on and assess performances from usually highly-talented young people, and to meet their teachers.

I became a regular at some of these schools, knowing, for example, that one of them would always bring me a bacon bap at break-time, and that at another one I would be taken at lunchtime to the pub across the road for a glass of wine, a sandwich and a good old gossip about mutual friends in the musical profession.

One particular venue I visited was a real "perk", and I felt privileged to be allocated to it. This was almost a full week examining at schools in Jersey in the Channel Islands, and what a joy that was. There is quite a story attached to the beginning of my visit and Maureen laughs at herself every time I tell it.

We drove from our Halesowen home to Birmingham International Airport, where I was to catch the flight to St Helier, and Maureen drove back. I checked in, sat around waiting (I undoubtedly had a drink), took the flight, landed at St Helier, got in a taxi which took me to my hotel at Millbrook a little away from the town, checked in at the hotel, was shown to my room, changed, and then walked down to the beach, where I strolled back towards St Helier.

I decided to call home, to let Maureen know that I had arrived safely and was comfortably ensconced. She answered the phone and told me she had only just got home herself!

Driving away from Birmingham International she had got onto the motorway network but took the wrong turning at the M5 junction and found herself going south rather than north. Apparently she drove round Droitwich several times until at last she spotted a sign for Kidderminster, "Ah, I can do that," she thought to herself, so followed the road to Kidderminster, where she picked up signs for Halesowen and eventually got back home.

I really felt for her, especially as I was already having such a pleasant time. The hotel suited me down to the ground. It had no swimming-pool, no games-room or slot-machines ("we don't want to attract families here" the very urbane proprietor told me – this was just the kind of hotel Fawlty Towers would have liked to have been), it was quiet, it had lovely grounds, the cuisine was wonderful, the wine list was extensive and incredibly cheap (no VAT), so I really enjoyed beginning my bottle over a book in the blissfully genteel restaurant, and then taking the rest up to my room.

The standard of the examination candidates was very high, so I had great musical satisfaction as well as great hospitality. I also enjoyed exploring the all-glass Lalique church on St Aubin's Bay, and crawling through the neolithic burial mound at La Hougue-Bie, with the World War II German hospital built beneath it.

I had my own taxi-driver all week, Pat Green, who absolutely insisted on taking me everywhere once she learnt that I had reviewed a couple of Barry Manilow concerts she had flown all the way from Jersey to hear at Birmingham's National Exhibition Centre. I actually admire Manilow as a musician, as I do Neil Sedaka. Sedaka's songs were the sound-track to my adolescence (Happy Birthday, Sweet Sixteen – what a number!)

At the other end of the British Isles, Northern Ireland was the source of an hilarious anecdote. This was an examination carried out on video, but still had to be held under the strict conditions which applied to live examinations, so the performance had to be continuous and lasting no longer than 20 minutes.

I settled down to watch the performance. Halfway through, the candidate was wearing a different shirt! And the date in the top right-hand corner of the screen was one day later! I kicked the problem upstairs, and the moral is, if you're going to pull a fast one, cover all your tracks.

The Board decided to change its sight-reading requirements, and I was commissioned to compile a new book of tests, three (increasing in difficulty) for each instrument and voice. I really enjoyed doing this, having all the resources of the Birmingham Conservatoire library, plus my helpful students and eventually produced the book.

We had a meeting at base in Cambridge to go through it and all was approved, at the end of the afternoon I began the long drive back home. As the evening drew on I realised I was starving, and was so looking forward to a supper of burger and chips in the Amber Tavern in Quinton, washed down by a pint.

I arrived there at 8.05pm, went up to the bar, and placed my order. "Sorry, sir," smarmed the landlord, "we closed the kitchen at 8 o'clock and the chef's going home."

People who know me well will anticipate how I reacted, "I've just driven 180 miles in order to eat here and, as I'm a regular here, I want something now!"

I got my burger and chips.

There were about 80 of us examiners, divided into teams of six or seven. For some reason our team was designated the naughty team, as we were always accused of playing up at standardisation weekends, and we always won the pre-lunch quiz on a Saturday. One of my team-colleagues was Heather Fairs and I formed a close friendship with her and her baritone husband Alan, who always came with her. He sat in the lounge during the day, reading the papers and watching the rugby, then joined us at dinner. I bump into them at concerts occasionally, generally in Worcestershire (they live in Bewdley), and it's always lovely to see them.

Later I also became an examiner in Performance Studies (Drama, Dance and Music), and that was a different kettle of fish. Many of the teachers were failed performers who thrust their wannabe theatricality onto their pupils, and to be frank it was somewhat distasteful to observe.

I saw some amazing performances, including one girl in Lancashire (where the teacher took me out to a wonderful country pub every day for a barm-cake lunch) to whom I had no hesitation in awarding 100%. I also saw some terrible ones, where one wondered what on earth the teacher was doing entering and presenting them.

In one school in Birmingham, which put on a fantastic buffet lunch for me and my Team Leader, who was making the mandatory visit to moderate my marking, we witnessed the most atrocious, not-really-bothered, performance from a couple of students. "I can't give this more than 2%," I muttered to my Team Leader. "Go for it, Chris!" was her reply.

Another example of the negligent attitude of Performance Studies teachers came when I was sent to examine at a school in East London. It was an evening session so that parents could be present to observe the work of their children, which was fine. It was always good to have an audience there, as it always lifts the performers, but it would have been good to have had the teacher there, too.

But there he wasn't! He'd left all the organisation in the hands of the students themselves, even to the extent of their organising an interval buffet and drinks, as well as having to do their own performances. It was an outrageous dereliction of duty and of course I reported him.

In recent years all live examining has been stopped. Instead everything is now done online and that's not for me.

Being bilingual in English and Italian, I was also doing some work as a police and court interpreter. In some ways it was tedious, demanding and poorly paid, but there were some great stories, too.

My first-ever interpreting assignment came in the middle of the night, when I was awoken by a call at 3am. Could I drive over to Stechford police station now? Yes, of course I could, hoping it was a murder. I dressed, got into the car, and started to drive over to the other side of Birmingham, not really knowing how to find the place, but confident that I would be stopped somewhere along the way by a policeman wondering what I was doing out at that time of night, from whom I could then ask directions.

As Sodd's Law would have it, I didn't encounter one, but did manage to find my way there and went down into the damp, Stygian atmosphere of the custody cells, escorted by the WPC who had arrested a young Italian woman, working as a cook at a pub in Bearwood and who had apparently racially abused a Pakistani taxi-driver earlier that night as he drove her home.

She had no English (so how could the racial abuse be delivered, I now ask myself?), hence my presence. The interview progressed, me translating all the questions and translating back her answers and notes were made. And then one remark from the WPC drew from the accused, "That's-a bullshit!" So much for having no English.

After a caution from the custody sergeant (I learned always to call them "Sarge" as though I were a copper myself) she was free to leave, but not before inviting us all to her pub, where she would give us a meal if ever we appeared!

I drove back home, for a couple of hours' sleep before driving many miles up the M6 for an examining session in Wigan. *Che nottata*, as we say in Italian.

An even more entertaining assignment came one afternoon when I was summoned to the Digbeth police station, just by the Bull Ring. A young Albanian couple had been caught shoplifting in Rackhams, the swish department store behind Birmingham Cathedral, and no Albanian interpreters were on the police list. But the husband spoke Italian, hence my invitation.

We did the interview and it turned out that they were illegal immigrants (but that was ignored by the authorities, as the ramifications of charging them with that offence would have been huge). It was decided to progress no further about the shoplifting, so we went back to the desk in the entrance hall for them to be cautioned.

The desk sergeant was an old pupil of mine from St Paul's, Tessa Moyle. It was she who, one lesson, when I had told the kids they could bring in their own records to play and talk about them – every one of them predictably and understandably pop music, brought in the famous duet from Bizet's Pearl Fishers, and told us how it made her cry; and she it was who ran to my music room on a later occasion to tell me that my assistant, teaching her class, had flipped his lid (not her words) and I needed to come and rescue the situation, which I was able to do.

Tessa was a great girl. And now here she was, presiding at a desk where there was an Albanian couple crying, an afternoon drunk ranting and raving, and heaven knows what other mayhem going on. "Right!" she shouted, and pressed the On-switch of a cassette tape-player.

As the sounds of Gregorian chant wafted out, everything became calm, and business went quietly on.

When I told Terry Grimley about all this one day in the newsroom, he immediately announced a new television drama series, to be called (in an American accent) *Police Interpreter!*

Translating was another source of income and that demanded a different kind of concentration. When you are dealing with an arcane baroque opera text in Italian you have to keep every word in your head until you can come up with a convincing word-order in English, and it's not easy; I think I also did some similar translations from French and German, too.

From baroque opera to the house-magazine of an Italian shoe-manufacturer (too complicated to explain how that came my way), which was a very lucrative gig. The magazine was full of tributes to the company from their happy workers (no, this was Italy, not China), and I was bombarded with features which they wanted translated yesterday in order to send to their international traders. I did a couple of years of this, but I think the idea was subsequently kicked into touch, and was very disappointed never to receive any exquisite shoes either for myself or for Maureen, who needed a new pair of boots.

But as indicated above I had also begun teaching at Birmingham Conservatoire, initially with "Paperwork" to very small groups who needed additional coaching in theory. This came about through an approach from the Vice-Principal David Brock, who had been one of my closest friends at University (though as a lofty – apart from his diminutive height – PostGrad studying for a PhD he was older than the rest of us), and whose Best Man I was privileged to be when he married another university friend, Evelyn Williams.

My teaching commitments at the Conservatoire grew and grew, until in the late 1990s I was lecturing 14 or 15 hours every week, and I enjoyed it so much. So many talented students passed through my classes and it's a constant joy wherever I go today – CBSO, Orchestra of the Swan, Longborough Festival Opera, English Symphony Orchestra, and elsewhere – to see them performing with such aplomb.

I instigated a Criticism and Journalism class, which was very well attended, so much so that there was a follow-up hour for those who were really keen. I gave them examples of reviews of the same event to compare, reviews I thought were excellently written, reviews I thought were appallingly written, I got them to write their own reviews of events and told them all about the bits and pieces of how the system worked.

I also taught them about the importance of a well-constructed press release and how to target the designated recipient. Imagine, I said, if some idiot were to send me, a specialist and accredited music critic, a press release selling a Beethoven event, beginning with "Beethoven was a famous composer who became deaf". That would be rolled up and thrown into the bin immediately.

Some of these students were so talented in writing that I signed them up to join my reviewing team on the Birmingham Post, and several of these were not English but Scandinavian, with a perfect command of our language. One of them went back to Sweden to become a presenter on broadcast media there and I'm very proud that the seeds I sowed all those years ago have flourished so abundantly.

And then I made probably the biggest career mistake of my life.

*   *   *

Brainchild of the great violinist Yehudi Menuhin, who, whilst playing to fearful departing servicemen and broken returning ones during World War II had realised the therapeutic powers of music, Live Music Now! was a charity which enlisted the talents of emerging young musicians in order to enrich the lives of the sick, the elderly, the disabled and disadvantaged, indeed anyone physically unable to experience live musical performance in conventional venues.

So these talented youngsters played in hospitals, care homes, prisons, special schools, sheltered accommodation and other such environments. The musicians were all rigorously auditioned and assessed as to their ability to communicate with their various audiences, and as to how they would be able to involve them in live participation. It was a great idea.

There was a Midlands branch, with its office actually within Birmingham Conservatoire, but for various reasons it had great difficulty in making a success of things. When the then current director resigned I was flattered by the local

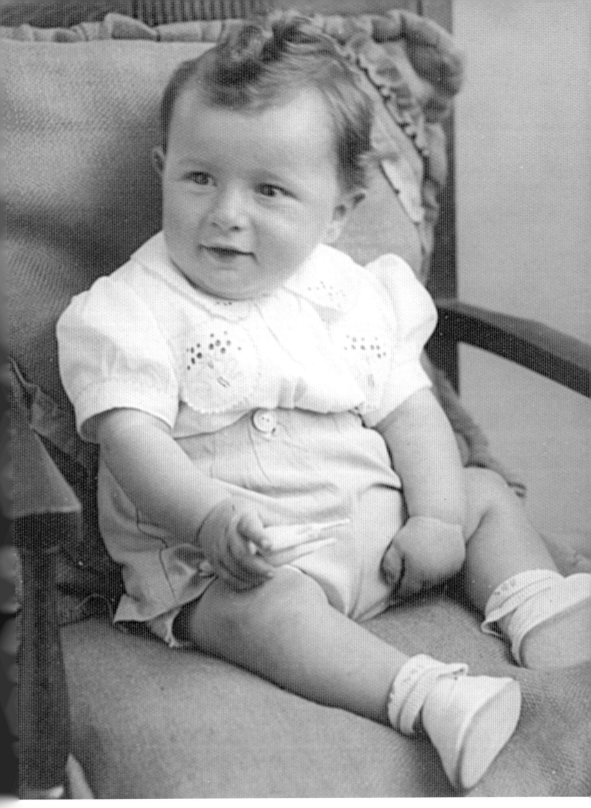

I won 10 shillings with this photo of me in Woman's Weekly.

Top: Mum, "To my dear husband". Says it all, in Italian. Dad on war service.
Bottom: A distant relative built the block on the left, named Palazzo Lemme and Mum was born there, where Dad courted her.

Right: Yuri Temirkanov's self-portrait.
Bottom: Leonard Bernstein's autograph, La Fenice, Venice, August, 1968.

Please hand in this ticket to the desk on the evening prior to departure.

bed   n.

room   n.

Beds are to be vacated by 9 30 a.m. on the day of departure but luggage may be left for the day at the desk.

Above: Lady Susana Walton in Facade – reciting Pomp.
Right: Birmingham Town Hall long before its restoration.

Above: Maureen and me at the 18th birthday party of one of my star pupil performers.
Opposite: Dress rehearsal of Love from Judy. I was directing as well as conducting.
Below: I was considered important enough to be interviewed in the local Rostov-on-Don press.

На орбитах дружбы и сотрудничества

ЖУРНАЛИСТУ АНГЛИЙСКОЙ ГАЗЕТЫ «БИРМИНГЕМ ПОСТ» В РОСТОВЕ ПОНРАВИЛИСЬ ОПЕРА, РАКИ И ВОДКА

А ПО ВОЗВРАЩЕНИИ ДОМОЙ КРИСТОФЕР МОРЛИ ПЕРВЫМ ДЕЛОМ РЕШИЛ ПРОЧИТАТЬ «ТИХИЙ ДОН»

На снимке: Кристофер Морли и главный дирижер Ростовского государственного музыкального театра Александр Анисимов.

Фото О. Бекаревой.

Julian Lloyd Webber.

Chair of Governors, with close Conservatoire connections, into taking on the job, assured that all the contacts I had in the local musical world would be of immense use.

This meant I had to give up all the Conservatoire teaching I loved so much, all the students who were so appreciative of my teaching, and turn to something in which I had no experience at all. But I was looking forward to the opportunity of working in a different way with talented young musicians in such a good cause, thinking perhaps of my own cousin who had Down's Syndrome, and knowing how he would respond to hearing a live musical performance.

It was great interacting with the performers, it was very moving witnessing the response of the audiences, such as one tiny lad who had no ears, shuffling himself up to the front of the room in a special school where a flute and guitar duo were performing, in order to watch fascinatedly and sense the vibrations and overtones.

Another rewarding experience was setting up a link between Live Music Now! and HM Prison, Winson Green, where I established a great relationship with the prison chaplain. As a result of that I was invited to the launch of a CD made by a few prisoners who had formed themselves into a rock group, and who wanted profits from the sale to go towards a Youth Centre, keeping vulnerable youngsters away from the temptations which had turned themselves into hardened criminals. That was amazing.

I also refashioned the procedure for auditioning new applicants to become performers on the scheme, actually making the audition process part of a live performance instead of just an arid run-through in front of a panel. I enjoyed all of this.

And I had a great triumph which made all my colleague regional directors envious when on Christmas Eve 1999 I secured Sir Simon Rattle's agreement to become the Midlands Patron of Live Music Now!, a title I think he still continues to hold.

Things were great on the artistic side of my Live Music Now! work, but I was finding the fund-raising onerous. I found going about the whole process was difficult, interfering with my natural creative and educational instincts, so in early 2004 I decided to resign.

Again, as when I took the decision to close Cottage Music, I felt a great weight off my shoulders. I had made some wonderful friends during my tenure, not least two highly supportive members of the Board of Governors, Frank Shaw and Ken Maslen, both sadly now no longer with us, and many of the young performers kept in touch, telling me of their progress both professionally and domestically. One particular duo, Bluesy Susie, seemed to be working nonstop, chiefly all around the

Welsh Marches (an area I love, incidentally), but they were also finding time to bring a family into the world.

I was so sorry to have lost all the teaching I loved at Birmingham Conservatoire, and of course there was now a considerable hole in my income, but there was a hopeful light beckoning at the end of the tunnel.

Though all my regular lectures had been re-allocated to other teachers during my five years away, I was invited back for special classes. Journalism and Criticism was revived, as was the Performance Class I enjoyed so much.

I was being paid to sit in the comfortable Adrian Boult Hall and observe live performances from some of the most talented young musicians in the country, and then comment on their stage presence and presentation.

There could have been no better return to the atmosphere where I felt so much at home. Birmingham Conservatoire was to remain a quiet but steady presence in my life for many years to come, and in fact was to provide me with one of the lasting highlights of my career.

Chapter 8

HOW AND WHY

Truth to tell, ever since 1988 it had been my writing for the Birmingham Post which was the major element in my professional life. The paper had an enviable reputation for its arts coverage, and was highly respected not only in this country but abroad, and I had the privilege of being its chief music critic.

I was assembling a great team of assistants around me, all of them hugely experienced in the musical world in one way or another, and together we were reviewing upwards of a dozen events a week, sometimes two or three pieces appearing on the same arts page the very next morning after the events.

The whole business of constructing and delivering a live review was packed with adrenaline. I know there are some critics who pride themselves on never making notes, but I scribble throughout a performance, jotting down reactions which will serve as an aide-memoire once it comes to polishing the review. Sometimes I can't even read these scrawls, but I have the comfort of knowing they are there.

And certainly anyone next to me, inquisitively peering over my shoulder, can't make anything out. I hate being cramped next to a stranger who may well be disturbed by what I am doing, who may be over-nosey, and who may actually be inhibiting the actual physical process of writing.

This is why I insist on seats at the end of a row (two seats, I stress, as I don't see why a reviewer should plough a lonely furrow when concert- and opera-going are meant to be social events), so that one arm is free to work and my companion on the other side knows what is happening. I also insist on complimentary programmes, as I don't see why I should be paying to subsidise the publicity I am giving to whichever enterprise I am reviewing. And if there is any hospitality going, I fully expect my guest and myself to be invited, along with any freeloading throngs.

Although I pay little heed (it's my review, after all), it's sometimes interesting to hear people's halftime comments (and occasionally to explain to dewy-eyed ravers why I think the performance we've just heard didn't go so well, something which happened very recently featuring a rising star at a concert in the area).

And I expect seats in a good part of the house as well, so that I can review from the best listening perspective possible. My CBSO seats at Symphony Hall are perfect for this. I'm not going to say I'm so lucky to have them, as they are vital for me to be able to do my job properly, and therefore I expect to have the use of them as a matter of course. They were also good for the critic's leap to the door to get onto the phone after a concert in the days of overnight reviews (more of that later).

Early on after my appointment as Chief Music Critic I went along to the latest monthly concert of a local chamber music society, and was put into a seat near the back where I could hear the crockery being prepared for the interval libations. I complained and was told, "oh well, you can move your chair. Your predecessor always used to!"

I firmly pointed out that I was not my predecessor, and that I expected better accommodation, not having to shift furniture. The organisers acquiesced and ever since that incident over 30 years ago, those two organisers and I have become very close friends, and I have supported that society in whatever way I have been able to, even to the extent of successfully endorsing grant applications they have made.

I was invited to speak at one of their anniversary dinners and was rewarded with the gift of a pair of musical socks!

All these strictures sound very harsh, but half a century of experience has confirmed in me the value of a reviewer's work, not just for the interested reader, but also as publicity for the performer and promoter. A well-qualified (and that adjective is essential) critic who is rigorous in every aspect of his work will earn the respect of everyone in the musical profession we all want so much to promote.

Anyway, back to the actual process. I would be scribbling notes all through the first half of the concert or opera, and during the interval I would be writing the first part of my review. There would be people anxious to come up to me and tell me what they thought of it all, in order to get their opinions to influence what I was writing, but one of the duties of whomever was accompanying me was to keep them at bay. Maureen became very good at that. And I still had my famous glare up my sleeve.

After the interval I would be doing three things at once: listening to what was happening, assessing what from that I was going to write about, and actually writing, all at the same time. What I had written during the interval wouldn't necessarily be appearing at the top of my review, as the most important part of the evening might still be yet to come, so I was juggling that, too. The most important part of the concert always had to appear first in a review, not least to avoid the depredations of a hapless subeditor who might have to make cuts for reasons of space, usually dispensing with the final paragraph. So much for the "begin with a fanfare, end with a cadence" advice I always gave to my students.

Though those disfigurements should never really have been necessary. Every week I used to send in a list of concerts coming up during the next seven days, what and where they were and who was covering them, and what the word count of each review would be, so the paper would know how much space to make available.

Because reviews generally had to be with the paper by 10pm, this meant I sometimes had to miss the end of a concert, which frequently happened at Symphony Hall with its 8pm starts so beloved by its director, my dear friend Andrew Jowett (he was eventually persuaded to see the light and begin at 7.30pm, but there were no overnight reviews by that time).

One particularly painful departure came when I had to leave before the finale of Beethoven's Eroica Symphony, Carlo Maria Giulini conducting the Philharmonia Orchestra in what was proving an amazing performance. I don't think the Eroica is the greatest symphony ever composed; I *know* it is, but there were several occasions when I had to miss the finale.

Another such time was when Kurt Masur brought his Leipzig Gewandhaus Orchestra to perform a cycle of all nine Beethoven symphonies at the opening of Symphony Hall's first complete season in September 1991.

Kurt Masur was a lovely man (only two years previously he had invited 3000 demonstrating citizens of Leipzig into his Gewandhaus to protect them from the desperately strutting Stasi police forces as the Iron Curtain was collapsing), and we had some great interviews together over many years. One of them was on the morning of the opening concert of this particular Beethoven cycle, an interview which I duly preserved on my little Panasonic dictaphone recorder (gosh, have I really had it that long?).

As the interval of that first concert came towards its end Maureen and I were making our way back to our seats, but we could hear announcements going on from the Tannoy, and they wouldn't stop. They were still going on as we sat down, with the concert about to resume.

And then the horrific penny dropped. This wasn't the Tannoy at all! It was my little dictaphone which I had inadvertently switched on whilst fumbling in my pocket during the interval and was now playing back my interview with Herr

Masur. What a tribute both to this tiny little machine and to the acoustic of the auditorium. Maureen took great delight in standing up and pointing down at me to indicate to everyone who was the culprit.

The end of every concert or opera was a hectic time. By now the review was completely written, and the task now was to find a telephone, which was not always so easy. Established concert-halls like Symphony Hall, Birmingham Town Hall and Birmingham Conservatoire's Adrian Boult Hall were not a problem, and there were many other enlightened venues which made an office phone available. I even remember the lovely manager of the wonderful Radnorshire Arms in Presteigne (now sadly defunct) vacating his office for me so that I could dictate my review after a Festival event – and it would be available in copies of the Birmingham Post in the supermarket just down the High Street of that sleepy little town in the Welsh Marches next morning.

Here's how it used to go. Dial the operator; on response, ask to make a transferred charge call to 0121 236 3366; when the paper's switchboard answered, ask for "Copy", and then wait your turn.

The girls (I only remember a couple of blokes) on Copy were amazing. They were there, sat at their typewriters, headphones on, ready to take copy from anything from arts reviews, House of Commons debates, sports events, whatever. I remember one time I was in the middle of dictating a review when the copytaker said, "Sorry, Chris, I've got to stop you. The greyhound man is on, dictating the latest result from Hall Green!"

They were fantastic. You would announce who you were, what you were reviewing and where, and then begin dictating, three or four words at a time in a natural rhythm, and obviously dictating all punctuation and subsequent capital letters as well. Dictating was quite an art and I really enjoyed it, both my own expertise in delivering (despite my stammer) and the telepathic skills of the copytaker at the other end. I established warm relationships with all of them, and one of them even became a Cottage Music customer, buying things for her children.

Technical words and foreign names had to be spelt out using the A-for-Alpha, B-for-Bertie method, as these lovely girls couldn't be expected to understand the intricacies of words like "Sprechstimme", for example. It was all part of the fun, and at the end of the process we, at both ends of the telephone line, felt we'd achieved a job well done.

But sometimes there were howlers. One rainy Friday night in Bromsgrove (that sounds like the title of something) I was reviewing a string orchestra concert in a church on the fringes of the town. At its conclusion I went out to look for a telephone box (this was long before the days of mobile phones), and eventually found one really out in the wilds. Half of its windows had been smashed by the local intelligentsia, and the person before me had obviously used it as a public convenience. But it was a connection to civilisation in the form of the Birmingham Post copydesk.

I dictated my review and at one point, referring to the performance of a concerto by Vivaldi, I felt I ought to spell out "Caps V for Victor lower-case i, v for Victor" and so on.

Next morning the review appeared, including a mention of the A minor Concerto by Victor Vivaldi. My mother once tried to teach me to dance to the music of Victor Silvester, with little success...

On another occasion I was at Birmingham Hippodrome, reviewing a Welsh National Opera production of Puccini's Turandot. In my piece I described how in the first act we were all concerned for the fate of a hapless Middle Eastern prince on his way to execution after having failed to answer the three riddles set by the steely-hearted princess.

Next morning I read how we had all been moved by the execution of the Prince of Pershore.

Think about it.

*   *   *

Those were incredibly happy times. My contract stipulated that I had to appear in the newsroom once a week, and how I loved that. The atmosphere buzzed, everyone on fire with producing copy, and everyone so supportive of each other. These hardened journos who were there all day every day took to me so kindly, and I relished every minute of it.

I rubbed shoulders with all levels of the structure, from the Editor, through the subeditors and the various specialist correspondents, and right on to the lovely copytakers. It was great.

One morning when I was in there the news came through that the Queen's favourite bandleader had just passed away, and what headline should we use? Some wag sent a suggestion all around our computers: "Dead Loss!"

I've already described the sense of working under pressure when an important piece was holding up the presses (my Jose Carreras interview), and the hush of a deserted newsroom very late at night when only an arts reviewer and the brilliant cartoonist were working, while the presses were thundering in the basement rolling out the early editions. It was a world I loved and felt so thrilled to be part of.

Now all of that has gone. Everything is done online, so there is not even any need to go into the premises. I haven't set foot inside the door for around 15 years, and none of us can put a face to a name anymore. Yes, this is progress, but it's very sad and dehumanising.

* * *

Why go through all this process? What is the point of an arts review? After all, the event is dead and gone, so who needs to know about it?

Well, everybody. We look forward to reading the report of a soccer, cricket or rugby match, to finding out the result, who played well, who wasn't on such good form, what the atmosphere was like, and so on.

It's exactly the same with a concert, an opera, a ballet or a play. It's an event that happened, and as such, it's worth chronicling. This is the first function of a review, to say that the event took place.

How did the sportsmen perform? How did the artists deliver? This is the second function of a review, to report on presentation standards. So, so far we have "Last night there was a recital from Walter Plinge of piano music by Chopin. The soloist played with a crystal-clear technique and subtle pedalling."

The third and final reason is the most difficult to explain. If the reader trusts the reviewer they will be interested to learn how they personally reacted to the performance. If the reader was also there, then of course comparisons can be made; and even if they weren't there, they will feel that the reviewer has brought the event to life and painted a picture in words.

So now we might have this: "Last night there was a recital from Walter Plinge of piano music by Chopin. The soloist played with a crystal-clear technique and subtle pedalling. I felt, however, that some of the gaps between movements were too long, allowing the tension to sag, when Chopin's works were always conceived all of a piece."

Here we now have the reaction of someone who knows his Chopin, who knows how he composed, and who is unafraid to put his own response on the line. Incidentally, there is nothing wrong with referring to oneself in the first person, despite the convention which persisted for well over a century that the critic should remain anonymous, and use only the royal "we". The first step towards humanising reviews was the introduction of the use of the critic's initials as a byline, instead of a fancy sobriquet (I have seen some really naff reviews penned by people calling themselves "Music-lover", for example). Then, at last, full identification came in, which was like a breath of fresh air.

A couple of paragraphs earlier I wrote about the reader trusting the reviewer. Very early on in my tenure as chief music critic of the Birmingham Post someone wrote to the paper complaining about the apparent impertinence of some comments by "a tyro of a music critic". In those days the Letters Editor would invite us to add a paragraph of response at the bottom of such a letter, and so I pointed out that I was well into my fifth decade, had already been reviewing for nearly 20 years, and had had the benefit of a fairly decent education in music. That chap subsequently became quite a follower, and hung on to my every word!

I could have shown off in all my reviews by using high-flown technical terms to flash my knowledge around (and that would have been an economical use of space, too, one piece of jargon eliminating the need for a more wordy description), but that would have been anathema in a newspaper aimed at the general reader.

Blinding the reader with science would be discourteous, making the non-expert feel inadequate and a failure, and would stifle their enthusiasm. By all means use esoteric jargon in more specialised publications, but not in newspapers. We do not want to discourage anyone showing an interest in our subject. I think the job of a ballet reviewer, with all the jetees and entrechats and so on, is far more difficult than mine, but the point remains.

One last thing to round off this chapter of technicalities.

Everyone will have seen the quotes on hoardings and theatres, and in newspaper advertisements, such as "Fred Nurk's Hamlet is the best I have ever seen."

What the reviewer may well have written was "I wish I could say Fred Nurk's Hamlet is the best I've ever seen, but I'm afraid it wasn't, for the following reasons."

Now on to the next chapter, and one of the best orchestras you could ever hope to hear.

Chapter 9

CBSO ON TOP OF THE WORLD

My appointment as Chief Music Critic of the Birmingham Post in 1988 could not have come at a more exciting time. Simon Rattle had been at the helm of the City of Birmingham Symphony Orchestra for eight years, and under his tenure the orchestra was rising to a crest of a wave where it remains to this day.

When I first heard the orchestra in 1966 it came over as a worthy but somewhat pedestrian ensemble under Hugo Rignold and Harold Gray. There seemed to be performances of Richard Strauss' Don Juan and Brahms' St Antoni Variations on alternate fortnights, but there was the occasional highlight which still lives in the memory.

Harold Gray gave us Nielsen's Fifth Symphony, and we students perched in our cheapo seats in the choir stalls could observe at very close range percussionist Doug Milne's unstoppable attack on the improvised side-drum cadenza in the first movement. In another concert we could hear Stephen Bishop growling his way through the solo part of Richard Rodney Bennett's Piano Concerto; Bishop later changed his name to Bishop-Kovacevic in honour of his Yugoslavian mother, and subsequently dropped the "Bishop".

Then there were the Birmingham premieres of Mahler's Fifth and Sixth Symphonies, both conducted by Antal Dorati, and each one requiring an epic nine hours of rehearsal.

There had been the thrill of Louis Fremaux' first visit to the orchestra, with the Berlioz Symphonie Fantastique (oh, don't I have a problem with that piece!), and his return the subsequent year with an amazing Holst Planets; I still remember how he hurled out a particular key-change in Mars, and I made a point of incorporating his stance at that moment into my own conducting body-language.

Fremaux was of course a brilliant conductor of music from his French homeland, but he was also an expert exponent of English music. He was particularly adept in the music of William Walton, responding to the composer's innate clarity of line and luminosity (the sunlit Mediterranean had lapped so seductively during all Walton's adult life), and made several recordings with the CBSO which have remained benchmarks to this day.

Britten was another of Fremaux' revered English composers and a performance with the CBSO of the Rimbaud song-cycle Les Illuminations with Britten's professional and personal partner Peter Pears as tenor soloist remained one of the French conductor's most treasured memories throughout his long life.

In fact in 1978 Louis Fremaux was about to record Britten's War Requiem with the CBSO (many of whose players would have performed in the work's premiere at Coventry Cathedral sixteen years earlier) and Chorus, and the first recording in this country since the composer's own, when everything collapsed over the Arthur Baker debacle.

This was an accident waiting to happen, ever since Fremaux had committed himself so much to the CBSO that he made Arthur Baker, the orchestra's general manager, his own manager and agent. A dispute arose between the players and management over the recruiting and placement of viola personnel in a forthcoming Tippett performance (ironically, another English composer this Frenchman loved), and Fremaux, desperate to remain loyal to his agent, found himself painted into a corner, and had no choice but to resign.

It was a huge blow to the orchestra (there are some players from that period who still spit feathers at the mention of Fremaux' name I'm afraid – and to their shame) and to the city. All this happened just before the final concert of the season (Brunnhilde's Immolation from Wagner's Gotterdammerung and Stravinsky's Rite of Spring), and of course before the much-anticipated War Requiem recording.

A replacement conductor was found for the concert, who substituted a Scriabin work for the Stravinsky and the atmosphere was decidedly depressed. Even more worrying was the fact that a complete cycle of Beethoven symphonies to be conducted by Fremaux had been scheduled for a few weeks' time and was already virtually sold out. How could it be rescued?

After frantic efforts from what remained of the CBSO back-office staff the veteran Swiss conductor Erich Schmid was engaged and his Beethoven cycle was a triumph, because of his immense musicianship, his rapport with a grateful orchestra (he held the fort until Simon Rattle's appointment and then became the CBSO's first-ever Principal Guest Conductor), and also the huge emotional relief that this immediate problem had been solved.

Schmid had been a pupil of Schoenberg. My father, dabbling in the fashionable hobby of tracing his family tree, found out that he had relatives who had settled in the New World early on in the 20th century, and that the descendant of one of them was a musician who had studied in California with Schoenberg! She had died before we found all this out, otherwise I would have been on the first plane to the States to record all her memories of this composer I admire so much.

As for the planned War Requiem recording, it did happen a few years later and of course in the Great Hall of Birmingham University, with Simon Rattle at the helm. I was there at one session to write a piece for Arts Report, and I hope I captured the significance of the occasion. Soloists were the soprano Elisabeth Soderstrom, tenor Robert Tear and baritone Thomas Allen.

My abiding memory of that evening was of Bob Tear singing Britten's setting of the Wilfred Owen poem beginning "One ever hangs", performing with his arms outstretched as though crucified. Just listen to that heartbreaking track.

I never met Bob, though I found his autobiography Tear Here hugely entertaining and perceptive. I did have tea once with Elisabeth Soderstrom at her family home in Stockholm (more about that later), and had a lovely interview with Thomas Allen over a toasted sandwich lunch at the Marriott Hotel in Birmingham before a rehearsal of a fantastic concert-performance with the CBSO under Rattle of Mozart's Don Giovanni he gave alongside Willard White (whom I once interviewed in his temporary flat in Glasgow one incredibly rainy Sunday morning, empty bottles everywhere after the last-night party following Scottish Opera's Die Walkure, Willard singing Wotan).

Though we must never forget the importance of Louis Fremaux' work with the orchestra, raising its profile and making it a presence to be reckoned with in the recording studio, it was Simon Rattle who really put the CBSO firmly centre-stage worldwide.

Simon Rattle

The 18 years of Rattle's principal conductorship were heady times, with the orchestra's recorded repertoire tumbling out success after success, its touring availability so much in demand, its appointment of composers-in-residence (Mark Anthony Turnage was the first) so brilliantly successful, and building an audience base which must have been the envy of every other orchestra in the country, not least the patchily-attended London orchestras. There was also much television exposure which made Simon Rattle and the City of Birmingham Symphony Orchestra household names.

It was during Rattle's tenure that the renowned Birmingham Contemporary Music Group was founded as the result of a late-night conversation between two

CBSO cellists, Ulrich Heinen and Simon Clugston, on the coach returning from an out-of-town performance of Beethoven's Eroica Symphony, once the most gritty piece of contemporary music in existence. I was there almost at the birth of BCMG, and have seen it grow from a slightly gauche newcomer to one of the world's most respected such ensembles.

1990 marked the 10th anniversary of Rattle's official appointment as Principal Conductor of the CBSO and the Birmingham Post published a four-page supplement in celebration of the occasion. I collected quotes from various luminaries who had worked with him, including one from Kenneth Branagh, who had played the title role and directed a new film version of Shakespeare's Henry V, for which Rattle and the CBSO performed Patrick Doyle's specially-composed score. Maureen was beside herself when the fax from Branagh arrived all the way from Los Angeles.

In that supplement I also wrote words to the effect that we grumpy old wiseacres had ten years previously imagined the hardboiled members of the CBSO not relishing a 25-year-old whippersnapper teaching them how to suck eggs, and I went on to admit how wrong we had been.

The orchestra loved Rattle, and he loved them. He once told me that he was reluctant to take on another orchestra (as many conductors did) as he didn't believe in bigamy. Later on he did become one of the principal conductors of the recently-formed Orchestra of the Age of Enlightenment, but that was all to the good, as it enabled him to bring to the CBSO style so many elements of "period" performance (such as in that Don Giovanni presentation).

Having just mentioned the Orchestra of the Age of Enlightenment, I can't leave that fantastic ensemble without referring to a couple of memories: Mark Elder, returning with the OAE to the Symphony Hall he had helped open when he was principal guest conductor of the CBSO, for a tremendous account of the rare Donizetti opera Linda di Chamounix; and some years after that, Simon Rattle bringing the OAE to "his" Symphony Hall for a programme including Mozart's Symphony no.40 in G minor.

That symphony was the first Mozart symphony I had ever heard on disc (an LP from World Record Club to which I subscribed when I was a sixth-former), and it was that which eventually resulted in my BMus dissertation. It is the most mind-blowing piece, but you hear it too many times, and more often than not it is just merely churned through.

Rattle and the OAE restored it to the shattering significance Mozart penned into the score, and I wrote as much, saying that this symphony should be heard only once every ten years, and this would be the performance to deliver it.

But to return to Simon's time with the CBSO. He and I had frequent encounters, either individually or in press conferences (ghastly things, all the young wannabes or old has-beens trying to score points; in a way the old has-beens who have never been there – and always non-musicians, it occurs to me! – are the worst), and I remember a couple of revealing things he told me.

"I wish the players could read off a one-page score, so they wouldn't have to turn the page, but could instead keep their eye on the conductor all the time," he said.

And then once, when we were discussing the recently-released CBSO recording of the Rachmaninov Symphonic Dances (set down, I think, in the Maltings at Snape, just outside Aldeburgh) he told me that that was the first time he felt he'd "found" the CBSO sound, and I think I know what he means: a crystal-clarity surrounding an inner warmth in the strings. He also told me they'd recorded the filler, the Rachmaninov Vocalise, totally spontaneously.

That wonderful recording, which I cherish, was unfortunately released simultaneously with versions of the Symphonic Dances from Andre Previn conducting the London Symphony Orchestra, and Vladimir Ashkenazy conducting the Concertgebouw Orchestra, and all the London (I refuse to call them "national") critics concentrated on those two releases.

The personal hurt I felt then on behalf of the CBSO was a reminder of how I'd felt when two releases of Walton's First Symphony were issued simultaneously, one by Sir Malcolm Sargent conducting the Philharmonia, the other by Andre Previn conducting the LSO. It was Previn who got all the attention, and not my then hero.

Simon was always bubbling with ideas. One of these was "Towards the Millennium", a scheme conceived with Michael Vyner, musical director of the London Sinfonietta, when Rattle was sharing a taxi with him in a journey across Birmingham. The idea was to explore the music of every decade of the 20th century year-by-year as we neared the end of that century and dipped our toes into the 21st.

It was a brilliant scenario and the programming brought us so many gems trawling through key works of the disappearing century. A spin-off from this idea was "Leaving Home", a seven-part series for television's Channel Four, devised by Michael Hall (I still cherish the book), and again, an example of the exposure Rattle and the CBSO were deservedly receiving.

All of this was wonderful, but it meant I was really being kept on the ball. Terry Grimley, the indefatigable (he hated me using that word – but this is my book, boss) Arts Editor was red-hot in all the arts, theatre, graphic, music, and he really kept us on our toes as to what was happening.

Terry and I worked so well together. He and I were once at a Birmingham Festival Choral Society concert at Birmingham Cathedral and I was busy writing my review, which I completed ten minutes after the end of the concert, and which I needed him to send to the paper as I was jetting off somewhere early next morning. While I was writing he expressed his admiration to Maureen, saying "I don't know how he does it".

Well, I was and remain equally admiring of his ability to keep his finger on the pulse of everything going on in the world of the arts and still be a caring paterfamilias. He used to love nothing more than doing the family ironing whilst listening to a Nielsen symphony (I am typing this whilst listening to the world's greatest piano concerto – Brahms Two, if you didn't already know!).

The London critics hated the fact that the country's most exciting young conductor was firmly rooted in what they considered a second-rate backwater in the provinces ("provincial" actually is a word which is firmly banned in these parts; "regional" is okay, and we use "metrocentric" as a word expressing contempt for all things London-obsessed; this is a fact).

They could not understand why Simon Rattle had not already dumped the CBSO and headed towards the bright lights of one of the London orchestras. Up here we shook our heads sadly at the fact that they refused to recognise that Simon was building the best orchestra in the country and one of the best in the world.

To be fair, some of them did come round to see the light and they became regular visitors to Symphony Hall (which they acknowledged is an infinitely greater concert-hall than any in London) to hear the CBSO and indeed other visiting orchestras. Andrew Clements, chief music critic of the Guardian, always prefers to choose to come to Symphony Hall from his Oxford home should the same event also be being presented at the Barbican or on the South Bank. He and I have become good friends and colleagues.

Simon always responded to their blandishments with an air of surprise that anyone should expect him to give up his wonderful orchestra here for one of the pressurised London ones. Here we all shared in a sense of "family" with Simon, tousle-haired, all pepper-and-salt, as its head. The CBSO and Symphony Hall were a huge source of pride for Birmingham and its citizens, even those who knew little about music.

This incredible relationship endured for 18 years, comparable with Barbirolli at the Halle and Karajan at the Berlin Philharmonic, and Seiji Ozawa at the Boston Symphony Orchestra, though there was so much sourness there. But Rattle, wisely, came to the conclusion that it couldn't go on forever with the risk of becoming stale and predictable, and so he announced he would be leaving the orchestra at the end of the 1998 season.

This was a blow to everyone, but we soon realised that we had to move forward. Who to succeed Rattle? I published a wish-list, which included Valery Gergiev, Ilan Volkov and others, but failed to consider an outsider coming up on the rails.

A few months before Simon announced his retirement I had done a telephone interview with a conductor unknown to me who was due to conduct the Berlioz Symphonie Fantastique with the CBSO. His name sounded Japanese, but in fact he was Finnish.

Sakari Oramo proved a delightful interviewee, and obviously a more than delightful conductor of that concert (it being that particular piece, I delegated an assistant to review the evening), as after that the players went berserk, urging the management to secure him as Principal Conductor.

The management were avid too, and Chief Executive Ed Smith (he who had brought Rattle to Birmingham) and Concertmaster Peter Thomas flew to whichever Scandinavian location Oramo was in at the time, to make him the offer. And, after much thought, he accepted.

Sakari Oramo

In some ways Sakari was easier to rub along with than Simon, who had always held back a little. Sakari was more outgoing, such as when the CBSO was performing in Cologne and he, Ed and I had an outdoor lunch together at a place near the magnificent Cathedral (where I thought I was going to die, halfway climbing up the amazing tower) and when later that evening, after the concert, I had dinner with him, his parents, Ed and a few others, in a little restaurant by the railway station.

He was also more prepared to enjoy his family in public, such as the time he and his wife, soprano Anu Komsi (coincidentally, his predecessor Simon had a soprano wife – Elise Ross – as did Andris Nelsons, his successor – Kristine Opolais), brought their elder son's primary school classmates over from Finland to England to sing at the Elgar Birthplace in Lower Broadheath, just outside Worcester.

I of course went there to write it up. Maureen and I were having lunch beforehand in the garden of the Plough, the wonderful pub next door, and there were Sakari and Anu, heroically marshalling all the children.

Sakari was quite an amazing musician. Simon had shyly reappeared as a pianist, playing alongside Elise and the Birmingham Ensemble in a Sunday afternoon concert at Symphony Hall, but Sakari, whose career had been launched as Concertmaster of the Finnish Radio Symphony Orchestra, always travelled with his violin, and occasionally took it out of its case for performances.

There was a CBSO performance of Mozart's Symphony no. 39 in E-flat. K543, the first of the miraculous trilogy of symphonies he composed in six weeks during the summer of 1788, and during the final repeat of the Trio in the third movement I heard delicious ornamentations going on between the two clarinets.

With the permission of Rachel Blackman, the CBSO's press officer with whom I had a great working and friendly relationship, I raced up to the Green Room corridor during the interval and knocked on Sakari's door. "Who wrote those fantastic ornamentations?" I asked. "I did," he twinkled modestly.

Sakari of course brought us much Nordic music, including a complete cycle of Sibelius symphonies released on the Erato label (in competition with an earlier cycle from the CBSO under Rattle – there were rumours of a rivalry between them, fuelled by their wives), and I particularly treasure his recording with the CBSO of the Grieg Symphonic Dances.

But he was also a huge advocate of English music, not least the works of the neglected John Foulds, which resulted in a mini-revival of interest in that enigmatic composer's music. He gave us a memorable Elgar Third Symphony (Anthony Payne's miraculous elaboration of the sketches Elgar had left at his death), and over an astonishing weekend, all three great Elgar oratorios – the Dream of Gerontius, the Apostles, the Kingdom – on consecutive evenings. Didn't the CBSO Chorus cover itself in glory! There was also a tremendous concert performance of Britten's Peter Grimes, every nook and cranny of Symphony Hall used to amazing aural effect.

It was during Sakari's tenure that I reached my 60th birthday, and thanks to Rachel Blackman's prompting, I was made an honorary member of the CBSO and given a long-service award, a photograph of Sakari rehearsing the orchestra in Symphony Hall, with signatures and messages around the four borders of the frame from everyone working with the CBSO.

I was to receive a similar treasure, a huge framed photograph of Symphony Hall and Birmingham Town Hall in its newly-restored glory, presented to me by Andrew Jowett and Fiona Fraser (the wonderful press officer at Town Hall and Symphony Hall), on the occasion of my 25th anniversary as Chief Music Critic of the Birmingham Post. There was no-one left at the paper itself to remember the significance of the occasion.

But to get back to Sakari. He did wonderful things with the CBSO, building upon what Simon had achieved, taking the orchestra forward in a slightly different direction, and then stunned us all by resigning after ten years in 2008. He took up appointments back home in Scandinavia, but has since become the hugely respected Principal Conductor of the BBC Symphony Orchestra, following in the footsteps of two of his CBSO predecessors, Adrian Boult and Rudolf Schwarz.

We were all sorry to see him go, as we had been with Simon. And again, there was the question, who could follow that?

Andris Nelsons

The search was underway. The Venezuelan Gustavo Dudamel came to guest-conduct very impressively and I immediately received emails from some players begging me to use my influence (ha!) with the management to persuade them to engage him as Principal Conductor. But he was already going elsewhere.

Birmingham's gracious and historic Town Hall was about to re-open after years of refurbishment behind closed doors, restored to its original layout (the one Mendelssohn would have known) with only one gallery, lowered to reveal the full length of the magnificent windows, but also now equipped with an acoustic canopy, transparent so that we could still see the ceiling in all its glory. During the restoration all kinds of fascinating long-hidden features were discovered, including workmen's graffiti on a forgotten staircase down in the depths of the building.

The Town Hall now had its equivalent of Symphony Hall's Green Room/Director's Lounge. This was the Hansom Room, at the end of a long corridor, stuffed with sofas and flouncily-curtained. I immediately christened it "the Victorian brothel". An en suite was installed for when the Prince of Wales and the Duchess of Cornwall were to come for the official opening, and something which has provided a good conversation-piece ever since.

So much for the accoutrements, the important thing was, how was the sound? A private performance by the CBSO in the Town Hall was arranged, and conducting it was a 28-year-old Latvian who was currently in charge of a minor orchestra in Germany.

There were only a handful of listeners present, but they, as well as the members of the orchestra were galvanised as soon as the conductor burst into the opening bars of Strauss' Don Juan. Yes, that old warhorse that the orchestra had churned through so many times in this very building four decades earlier, but now revitalised under the baton of this young man.

During that weekend the CBSO recorded the Tchaikovsky Violin Concerto under this conductor, with his compatriot and ex-schoolmate Baiba Skride as soloist, and by the end of that weekend the feeling was unanimous: Andris Nelsons must be appointed as the orchestra's new Principal Conductor and Musical Director.

And he was. It was like the burning of the white smoke at a Papal Conclave, and the thrill in the air was palpable. Everyone was desperate to see him in action, and in fact a "get-to-know-you" Sunday matinee concert at Symphony Hall was soon arranged.

But before that there was a lunch at Bank in Brindley Place (actually on the Sunday of my 60th birthday weekend) hosted by Stephen Maddock (Chief Executive of the CBSO) and Rachel Blackman, for Terry Grimley and me to meet this exciting conductor.

My Dad and his partner Eileen were up here in Halesowen to spend my birthday weekend with me and Maureen, and we had gone to my comfortable local, the Bell and Bear on Gorsty Hill, for my usual Sunday lunchtime drink with Richard Lisseter, my best friend since we first met in 1974. I left them in Richard's care and drove into Birmingham for this memorable lunch.

Andris ate two steaks! And then, when dessert-time came, I couldn't finish the very large creme brulee I was brought, so he finished it off for me. This was a warmly bonding occasion, and Andris and I developed a close relationship, often texting each other about things.

The CBSO and the audience loved him. His body-language onstage was criticised by some pundits as extravagant, but in fact it wasn't. It was a balletic response to the music under performance and every gesture was there at the service of the music and certainly not at the service of an ego he, unlike many other conductors, didn't possess.

Andris brought a new kind of fresh air to the CBSO and therefore to Birmingham. His boyish enthusiasm was irresistible, his rumpled dress-sense was endearing, and I think everyone subconsciously wanted to look after him. I even gave him a Birmingham A-Z, but I don't think he ever used it. He knew the way from his apartment in the Bull Ring Rotunda to Symphony Hall and the CBSO Centre, and that was enough.

His particular strengths were in late-Romantic music, not least in Richard Strauss and Tchaikovsky, and he made important recorded cycles of both composers. And I was able to make a shrewd point about his ability in the music of another composer.

One concert featured Bruckner's Third Symphony, the epitome of the alpine journeys so characteristic of his great works, and a triumphant bringing-together of the composer's veneration for both Wagner and Bach (incidentally, one thing I learned on my life-changing music course in Salzburg all those years previously was that Bruckner had studied counterpoint with Simon Sechter, who had also taught Schubert decades earlier).

To say it was a fabulous interpretation of this wonderful piece wouldn't be praise enough. The BBC was there to broadcast it live, and the performance was subsequently released on a CD given away with the BBC Music magazine (I play that often and have come to spot flaws in the playing of a certain section, but it remains and always will be a fantastic reading).

In my review of the concert I opined that on this evidence Andris Nelsons would develop into a great Wagner conductor, and I was soon proved right. Just a few years later Nelsons was on the podium in the legendary pit at Bayreuth for a Festival production of Lohengrin. The presentation was roundly panned for its staging (not least the predominance of rats everywhere), but universally praised for its musical values under Andris.

Andris gave us great Wagner concert-performances back here in Birmingham. It had become a tradition to end each season with an opera, and those included Wagner's Lohengrin (2010), Tristan und Isolde (2012), The Flying Dutchman (2013) and Parsifal (2015). Symphony Hall was the perfect space for these presentations, especially in the vaulting textures of Parsifal.

It took me a long time to grow to like Lohengrin (it was the same with Tannhauser), and I'm afraid I must be one of the few people in the musical world who are repelled by Tristan und Isolde. I have no problem with the adultery of the lovers, but I do have problems with the fact that everyone around them perishes as the result of their self-absorption; Wagner, you should not have projected your own situation so egotistically.

But The Flying Dutchman remains so significant to me after my experience at La Scala, and Parsifal is just too emotionally powerful to put into words.

One of my greatest hopes was that Andris would be contemplating a concert-performance of Wagner's Mastersingers, which would provide a wonderful showcase for the CBSO Chorus. I think it might have happened, but for one shattering event.

Andris announced he would be leaving the CBSO, going across the Atlantic to become Principal Conductor of the renowned Boston Symphony Orchestra. I felt this as a personal kick in the teeth, as Andris had so often told me he wanted to be here for the CBSO's centenary celebrations in 2020, and now here he was, leaving us after barely seven years at the helm.

Okay, Boston was an historic orchestra, had been associated with some great conductors, but was nowhere near the level now where it had once been, and nowhere near as high on the scale as the CBSO now was after the work of four amazingly talented and dedicated principal conductors. So why was Andris going?

I suspect it was a combination of the dollar-signs fruit-machining over in the eyes of his management, plus the fact that his then wife, Kristine Opolais, was obtaining an increasing number of engagements singing at the Metropolitan Opera in New York.

For many years in the past the CBSO had been looked upon as a stepping-stone towards a job with one of the London orchestras, and I have witnessed that happen (nowadays players actually come back to the CBSO, having experienced the hell-hole of working under London pressure, criss-crossing the city for commercial gigs before presenting themselves for an evening concert). But there had been a heartwarming link with players from the Bournemouth Symphony Orchestra, who came to the CBSO and stayed: Felix Kok, the hugely-respected concertmaster of the CBSO; Gwyn Williams, principal viola; Alwyn Green, bass trombone and euphonium soloist at the beginning of the orchestra's recording of Mahler's Seventh Symphony under Rattle, on an instrument borrowed in haste from his father in Norwich (the recording was set down in the Snape Maltings, at the other end of East Anglia).

But I resented the growing perception that the orchestra was now being looked upon as a stepping-stone for aspiring conductors as well. Why did Sakari leave after ten years? Why did Andris break his covenant to me and the audience and leave after only seven?

Much as I had loved Andris, I was pleased to read of the embarrassments he was being obliged to undergo in Boston. One example was having to pitch the first ball of the opening game in the Boston Red Sox' new baseball season, televised live (I've never known anyone less sporty). And then there were all the teas where he had to "make nice" (lovely American expression, though there aren't too many of those) with the blue-rinsed old dragons financing the Boston Symphony Orchestra and literally calling the tunes (think about that).

I was so pleased when he was appointed Kapellmeister at the renowned Leipzig Gewandhaus Orchestra. This is an orchestra dating back many centuries, steeped in gravitas and tradition, and there is no orchestra in the New World which can hold a candle to it. Andris was coming home.

But he hates flying. He spends his time on board listening to CDs, which helps alleviate the discomfort. I wonder how much longer he will be able to keep up this Atlantic-hopping, and at last see the light and return permanently to the European base where he belongs.

Mirga Grazinyte-Tyla

It was a long search to find a successor to Andris. In fact it went on and on and on, and people were becoming frustrated. I'd lost count of the times punters were coming up to me, asking if I'd heard anything and desperate to hear news.

I knew there was a short-list of possibles, all young conductors at the start of their careers, and I was uncomfortable with that. The securing of Simon Rattle had been a coup, the appointment of Sakari Oramo had been astonishingly imaginative, and the capture of Andris Nelsons, just when other organisations (such as the BBC Philharmonic Orchestra) were showing an interest was timely.

This was not the time, though, for the CBSO to put itself through the process of a here today, gone tomorrow principal conductor again. I was advocating the appointment of a conductor who had already established themself and was in no need of career-moves, and I named as possibilities the much-respected Jac van Steen (who had been at the helm of the BBC National Orchestra of Wales) and Andrew Litton (previously at the Bournemouth Symphony Orchestra, and subsequently in Dallas). I once did public interviews on the Symphony Hall stage with Andrew on two consecutive evenings prior to his conducting CBSO concerts, and he said, "hey, we ought to make a habit of this, the Chris and Andy show!"

People were really becoming impatient at the non-appointment of a new principal conductor, and there were fears that support for the CBSO might dwindle if such a state of uncertainty were to continue. The Chief Music Critic of the Birmingham Post was becoming increasingly concerned and indeed plagued by worried punters. What could I do about it? But I think I did succeed in doing something which helped.

Towards the end of July, just a few days after Andris Nelsons' last concert with the CBSO (which happened to be Beethoven's Ninth Symphony broadcast across the world from the Proms at the Royal Albert Hall), the CBSO wearily slotted in a late addition to its end-of-season concert schedule.

This was a strange programme, its first half consisting of Samuel Barber's Knoxville: 1915, sandwiched between movements from Tchaikovsky's Sleeping Beauty ballet, the second half devoted to Beethoven's Seventh Symphony.

When I read the name of the conductor (of whom I had never heard) I had visions of some wealthy Central European aristocrat who could afford to hire an orchestra in order to indulge her conducting hobby. I could not have been more wrong. The youngster who skipped onto the stage was elfin, smiling, and totally electrifying. This was Mirga Grazinyte-Tyla.

The first half of the concert was okay, but the Beethoven Seven in the second half was just mind-blowing, and believe me, I have heard some mind-blowing Beethoven Sevens (his most demanding symphony) from the CBSO, especially an unsurpassable one under an octogenarian Sir Charles Mackerras. And this was the equal of that.

But still the search (or was it prevarication?) went on, throughout the autumn and early winter of 2015. I decided to stick my neck out – after all, it was old and grizzled enough to lay itself on the block – and wrote a major article in the Birmingham Post, declaring that the orchestra must make a decision soon, and that Mirga Grazinyte-Tyla was the prime candidate.

A few weeks after that the announcement was made that this young Lithuanian had been appointed Principal Conductor and Music Director of the CBSO, and didn't we all rejoice! I went to the CBSO Centre for a long interview with Mirga, giving her a tiny jigsaw-puzzle of Symphony Hall as a "welcome" present, and we had a far-ranging conversation, during which she thrilled me by speaking of her interest in the music of Michael Tippett.

Her time with the CBSO has proved exciting, innovative (how many times have orchestral players been persuaded to sing madrigals?) and eventful. Audiences love her, as does the orchestra (though, ever since the time of Fremaux and Rattle there have always been some who grumble about the goose that lays the golden egg).

There has been one Mirga childbirth so far, with another on the way as I write (in fact a second son was born in August 2020), and great celebrations, spanning two seasons, had been devised for the centenary of the CBSO's founding in 1920. The coronacrisis lockdown of 2020 has put an end to all of that, and we are losing out on so many goodies from the orchestra, but there are far worse things happening at sea.

One festering sore remained. It was a long enough search to find a new Principal Conductor after Andris announced his departure. But the CBSO had been without a Concertmaster since the departure for health reasons of the universally admired, respected and self-effacing Laurence Jackson, over five years ago.

The obvious successor was treated shamefully by management and ignored. She has gone elsewhere, and is much missed here. Since then we have had a shuffling sequence of guest leaders, but they can never be Concertmasters in the true sense of the word.

A Concertmaster is the link between the members of the orchestra and the conductor (don't insult the role by describing it as that of a "shop steward"). Yes, it involves all the technical considerations of string-bowing, but, more importantly than that, it is the actual liaison with the conductor which steers the ship of the orchestra.

There were rumours of a school of thought among the management that a permanent Concertmaster was no longer needed, and that visiting freelancers would suffice.

I profoundly disagreed. During my tenure I have worked alongside Felix Kok, Peter Thomas and Laurence Jackson, and have always been made aware of their commitment to the orchestra and the nature of their relationship with whoever is on the podium – and especially with the Principal Conductor. We needed to have someone in place who would restore that partnership, and I sounded off in print many times about it.

And now, thanks perhaps in part to my pressure (as with the appointment of Mirga) the announcement has been made that we at last have a permanent Concertmaster, the Romanian Eugene Tzikindelean. He has guest-led the CBSO several times, including at a highly successful Prom concert conducted by Mirga, and takes up his appointment at the beginning of the 2020/21 season, the second half of the CBSO's centenary celebrations.

The power of the press?

Chapter 10

GLOBETROTTING

Being Chief Music Critic of a newspaper greatly respected for its long tradition of serious arts coverage has brought me invitations to review all kinds of events the length and breadth of Europe, and even on the other side of the world.

In this country I can number so many: the BBC Proms at the Royal Albert Hall; the Aldeburgh Festival (what a long drive, but worth it once you're there, particularly if you can get a room at the famous White Lion Hotel on the beach – with the smoke-huts where you can buy freshly-smoked kippers – and where the composer John Woolrich generously gave me the collective noun "a venom of critics" during a concert featuring the premiere of the Horn Concerto by the 100-year-old Elliott Carter, who gave a pre-concert talk); festivals in my beloved Welsh Marches (Ludlow, Presteigne); the anti-clockwise circuit of the Three Choirs (Gloucester, Worcester, Hereford), an annual festival I have grown increasingly to love after my angry young man's impatience with its air of self-satisfaction. Can I claim credit for the fact that thanks to my comments that stuffiness has disappeared from the set-up? I doubt it, but it has, and it's so good to see everyone smiling and helpful, and in my case, to feel welcomed by the festival conductors, who half-a-century ago seemed to feel they needed to keep themselves remote.

Apart from the triennial Three Choirs visit to Gloucester, there are other festivals in that Cotswolds county which figure largely in my itinerary: the Cheltenham International Festival of Music (today a sad shadow of its grandeur when I began reviewing and where I was introduced to Sir Arthur Bliss, Master of the Queen's Music); the amazingly enterprising Chipping Campden Festival organised by the energetic Charlie Bennett; and Longborough Festival Opera, which I have seen grow from its very beginnings in a converted barn into a well-equipped theatre with its own Bayreuth-style orchestra pit.

Longborough is quite a story. It has almost Cider with Rosie-like origins, with Martin Graham, visionary founder of the Festival, growing up in the Cotswolds, befriending the village elders and eventually consummating his passion for music with the creation of his own opera-house. It helped that he was a builder!

Martin and his wife Lizzie, and now their daughter Polly, are like a Cotswolds version of the Glyndebourne Christie dynasty – and even the Bayreuth Wagner dynasty! In fact Wagner is very much a feature of Longborough and in 2013, the bicentenary of the composer's birth, Longborough was the only company in the United Kingdom to produce a professional staging of the complete Ring cycle, and it was a triumph.

By this time Longborough was on the international reviewing circuit, and that all grew from me, and the years long previously when I had been the only critic from a newspaper of any stature to review their productions on a serious basis. It was from those reviews that the reputation of the company spread and critics began to arrive from both sides of the Atlantic.

That 2013 Ring cycle was the last time I saw my dear friend Michael Kennedy. Though he didn't know it, he was also my mentor, as he was (and remains) the music critic I admire above all others. He was the kindest and most generous of men, rigorous but gentle in his reviewing standards, and genuinely enthusiastic about the music under consideration. I shared his passion for Elgar, Wagner, Mahler, Britten, Walton, Strauss, though I have to admit I fell a little short when it came to Vaughan Williams, his first great love.

By 2013 he was very ill, but accompanied by his lovely wife Joyce (their personal story is a beautiful one) he managed to make it to Longborough. He was in the seat behind me for Die Walkure (his and my favourite opera in the tetralogy), and would often squeeze my shoulder when he wanted to discuss some particular point with me. He was a wonderful man and I will be returning to describe such happy times with him in a very different part of the world.

Almost on the verge of the Cotswolds is Stratford-upon-Avon, and for several years Shakespeare's town hosted a really vibrant Arts Festival. It was in reviewing many of those events that I began to work closely with Stephannie Williams, artistic director.

Steve is an amazing little bundle of energy. She knows everybody in the arts world (music, theatre, media), she has brilliant ideas, and she gets things done! The sponsorship she was able to cajole in order to bring the most illustrious performers to Stratford was quite staggering, and you can read all about her activities in so many spheres in her memoirs, *Beyond the Notes*, published by Brewin Books.

It was my privilege to collaborate with Steve in the writing of that book, and it is my privilege to have her now as my collaborator in the writing of this one.

She will pop up in the next chapter, and again at the very end of the book, but for now I'm going to move on to tours I was privileged to make with the CBSO and also with various local choirs.

It was always a thrill whenever the CBSO invited me to go on tour with them (always at the orchestra's expense, of course – the Birmingham Post wouldn't pay a bean, unlike some of the London papers and magazines who could afford to send their writers abroad from their own coffers). It offered the chance to bond with the players as well as the conductors, and I had some good plane-board conversations, such as one quite early on when I sat next to Peter Thomas, who asked me my assessment of the orchestra's string sections. And I told him.

There were other, less formal discussions, such as a long chat about the England cricket team with timpanist Peter Hill and co-principal viola Chris Yates. And then there were the pre-flight drinking sessions, not only in the airport departure lounge, but even in the coach going to the airport! Let me explain.

The CBSO has a pick-up system where coaches depart from various corners of Birmingham, collecting players who live along that particular route, and bringing them into the city. It works in exactly the same way when they are going to an airport in order to jet off on tour.

One of the pickup points is the junction of the Wolverhampton New Road and Hagley Road West in Quinton, just by McDonald's and opposite the Amber Tavern (well-patronised by some of the boys in the band), and that is where I, living in Halesowen, joined the coach. Just like on school trips, when all the miscreants piled onto the back seats, there on those seats were members of the brass and bass sections, armed with bottles of champagne and elegantly fluted glasses! Of course it would have been churlish to refuse their gracious invitation to join them in a drink to steady the nerves on the drive to Birmingham International Airport all those miles away.

It is the double-bass section that I have to thank for the scariest experience of my long life. We had flown to Helsinki for a concert in that city's new Finlandia Hall, and I had also enjoyed a visit to Sibelius' family home, Ainola, where he lived with his wife Aino and daughters from 1940 until his death in 1957. It is close to Lake Tuusula in Jarvenpaa, which is about a 30 minute drive from Helsinki, and was kept in the family until 1972, when it was turned into a museum.

Next day we made the Hydrofoil crossing across the Baltic to Tallinn, the capital of Estonia where the CBSO under Sakari Oramo were to perform a couple of concerts. During that crossing first violinist Philip Head, bassoonist John Schroder and I nerdishly compared our new-fangled Psion hand-held computer/word-processors. I was amazed at what John could achieve with his.

We arrived in Tallinn, and were installed in the sumptuous hotel which had been built to host the yachting competitors in the 1980 Moscow Olympics, just outside the medieval city walls. I took a stroll into the ancient centre and felt very much at home. Then there was the rehearsal and a reception with the British Ambassador in one of the ante-rooms of the concert-hall.

One of the bass-players said to me, "Chris, come and have a drink with us after the concert. We'll be in this bar," and he gave me the location and his own mobile number. I ought to point out that certain sections of the CBSO always sent out scouts a couple of days before any tour to identify suitable watering-holes.

It was a good concert and I made my way back to the hotel with many members of the orchestra to phone in my review back to Birmingham. And then I retraced my steps into the city for my tryst with the bass-players, found the bar – and they weren't there! The woman behind the bar told me they had gone on elsewhere.

I tried to ring the number I'd been given, but I was new to mobiles, and couldn't get the codes right. So I decided to cut my losses and find my way back to the hotel (the third time that day).

What had been a doddle in daylight was now a nightmare. I was totally lost, and had no idea where to go. Street-lighting was nonexistent, and I'd heard that muggings at night-time were particularly frequent in Tallinn. I was actually scared, which was a completely new experience for me.

Gradually I fumbled my way in what I thought was the right direction, and eventually heard two men talking at the bottom of a winding staircase. I decided I had to ask them for directions, and knew they would either help me or clean me out.

Of course I didn't speak Estonian, but decided to try German, and asked them the way to the, I think, Olympic Hotel. And bless them, they pointed me in the right direction instead of beating me up and robbing me!

When I arrived back at the hotel I was pleased to see the bar was still open, and there quaffing beers were Sakari Oramo, Stephen Maddock, Peter Hill and second violinist Michael Seal. I was so glad to see them and join them, and I told them my tale over a welcome half-litre.

For some reason they then started to sing Gilbert and Sullivan under Sakari's direction. "I'm a music critic," I said, and went to bed.

Meanwhile the bass section were happily downing beers back there in the scary city, totally oblivious of the anguish they had caused me.

On another trip I went with the CBSO and Sakari Oramo to Bucharest in Romania, where they were performing at the Enesco Festival. The concerts went very well (of course), I visited the museum in the Enesco House, and had my hair cut in the hotel barber's by a woman who could easily have been a steroid-ridden shot-putter representing Romania in any pre-Perestroika Olympic Games.

Came the morning of our departure and we clambered into the two coaches waiting outside the hotel. And waited and waited...

It seemed that some players had not settled their tabs at the hotel, and Richard Hawley (at that time orchestral manager, later Artistic Director of the Lichfield Festival, and eventually Artistic Adviser back in Birmingham's Town Hall and Symphony Hall – and looking like an Australian version of John Travolta) was having to clear all the accounts with his credit card.

We eventually set off for the airport, having lost a bit of time. There was a police escort and our coach went round a roundabout in the wrong direction on two wheels!

There was really no need for such histrionics, as we were still there in plenty of time, and the players bought everything on offer in the tiny duty-free shop. Their loved ones back home must have been charmed with all the pink wafer-biscuits brought to them (there was literally nothing else).

Our flight was to Innsbruck in Austria and we were all thrilled to be on a plane which was part of the Niki Lauda airline. Of course we all kept quoting the tired old joke to each other: "Who won the Formula One Drivers' Championship in 1975, 1977 and 1984?" "Lauda" "WHO WON THE FORMULA ONE..." etc.

Landing between the mountains at Innsbruck was a tremendous experience in its own right, but as we alighted the sparkling cleanliness of the alpine air just hit us, and I'm sure exhilarated us for days to come.

The CBSO were performing a new piece by an Austrian composer in what was actually a factory and a young soprano soloist was featured. She was a member of the CBSO Youth Chorus and in fact lived very near me. She flew over with her mother on the Thursday of the concert, ready to rehearse and perform the concert that evening and it was a wonderful performance.

Our local freesheet rag in my neck of the woods publishes on a Thursday, and when I got home a couple of days later I read a story saying how this local girl had "raised the roof" (the other cliché is "hit the right notes") in this performance with the CBSO in Innsbruck. The only problem was that the concert hadn't taken place at the time this slovenly piece of journalism was written.

Mother and daughter were flying just over a week after the 9/11 atrocity and planes were on huge alert. There could have been a disaster on their flight and yet this stupid story would already have appeared.

I took great pleasure in getting the paper into trouble with the Press Complaints Commission and I won't waste words in telling about the editor's weasel letter to me, "thank you for taking an interest in our newspaper".

My most recent trip with the CBSO was to Riga, capital of Latvia and Andris Nelsons' birthplace. He was bringing his orchestra back home and the atmosphere was wonderful. There were receptions, press conferences, television coverage and snow everywhere.

Riga is a beautiful city, with much art nouveau architecture to cancel out the Stalinesque monoliths, to experience it in the depths of winter was really something quite special. It was here where I acquired a taste for Balzams, a drink which tastes exactly as the name implies and one which shouldn't be allowed. I had a very bad experience with it one night on that visit and have gone very easy on it ever since, despite my lovely Belarusian neighbour, Oksana, bringing me back a half-bottle every time she goes home to Minsk.

I also went on tour with the CBSO Chorus, once when they went to Frankfurt to join Simon and the orchestra in Beethoven's Ninth Symphony, but most spectacularly when Kurt Masur invited them to be the Chorus in the Leipzig Gewandhaus Orchestra's performance of Mendelssohn's Elijah to mark the sesquicentenary of the composer's death in 1847.

Mendelssohn was important enough in Birmingham (where Elijah had been premiered), but he was God in Leipzig, where he lived, and where he founded the world-famous Conservatorium of Music, a role-model worldwide – including here in Birmingham.

This visit to Leipzig was amazing. I had started to sport a hat, so was a rather mysterious presence on the flight. At the piano rehearsal that evening the CBSO Chorusmaster, Simon Halsey, introduced me by saying, "In case you're wondering who the chap in the hat is, it's Christopher Morley from the Birmingham Post."

There was a round of applause, but the subsequent round of applause which then greeted Kurt Masur as he came in to take the rehearsal eclipsed all that. "My dear friends," he welcomed us all, and the rehearsal began.

It was electrifying and exactly as a rehearsal should be. He praised, he enthused, he got stroppy and we all worked – even the critic, scribbling notes. Afterwards we all agreed it had been a super evening.

Next day came the dress rehearsal with the Leipzig Gewandhaus Orchestra, and it was so energising. The CBSO Chorus were really on their toes (by the way, the performance was in the original English of the premiere in 1846), and I at last, reared on tired old tales of Victorian sentimentality in the work, revelled in the drama and immediacy of it all.

The performance was a triumph and afterwards there was a reception with a buffet and drinks. But that wasn't enough for some of us who found it difficult to come down to earth, so on the way back to the hotel we stopped at a little place which was still open, and where I had my first experience of Gluhwein.

There was time to kill the next day before the flight home, and I bought myself a copy of a lithograph of Clara Schumann, which is now pinned to the bookshelves and which faces me across my desk as I write.

This wasn't the first time I'd been with a choir to Leipzig. Previously I'd been a guest of the Birmingham Bach Choir when they travelled behind the Iron Curtain to perform Bach's great Mass in B minor in the composer's own St Thomas' Church in the heart of the city. The whole occasion was incredibly emotional artistically, and significant politically.

On our arrival Richard Butt, the august conductor of the choir, assembled us around the grave of Johann Sebastian Bach in the apse of St Thomas' and they sang a Bach chorale. Richard had tears in his eyes.

Next morning we rehearsed with the Leipzig Radio Orchestra and soloists, brought together by Christoph Biller, Bach's successor down the centuries as Kantor of St Thomas'. During a break I got chatting with Christoph and told him how I had fallen in love with the Variations and Fugue on a Theme of Mozart, by the Leipzig composer Max Reger, and that there wasn't a recording to be had in the United Kingdom.

That evening some of us were taken by various people connected with the church to a party in someone's home, driven in the battered old Trabants which were as much a symbol of the German Democratic Republic as the Morris Minors were of the UK. We were amazed and startled at how outspoken the people were in their criticism of the regime, and were terrified on their behalf that everything was being bugged by the Stasi. We were all aware that a charming "minder" had been assigned to us in our hotel, a lady who had once been an international athlete, pumped with steroids, but she was not with us in person on this occasion.

Next morning was the final rehearsal and Christoph Biller came up to me and presented a cassette-tape of the Reger Mozart Variations he had made for me overnight! I was so touched by that and I still treasure the tape (I listened to it in my bath when I arrived home, with a glass of whisky).

Later that morning I found a music shop where scores were so ridiculously cheap and I bought a score of the B minor Mass which I followed during that evening's performance.

During the afternoon the choristers were advised to have a siesta, but the secretary of the Birmingham Bach Choir and I escaped over to the impressive and historic Leipzig Railway Station and its huge bar for an excellent Stein of the local ale.

There was then a politically important teatime meeting with the Mayor of Leipzig. Among our party was Denis Martineau, one-time Lord Mayor of Birmingham and his lovely wife Mollie (they became very good friends and we met often at CBSO concerts); they were Presidents of the Birmingham Bach Choir.

Leipzig and Birmingham are twin cities and this meeting reinforced that connection, with warm speeches from both the Mayor and from Denis, who spoke so eloquently off the cuff. I liked Denis a lot, and he was so grateful to me when I tipped him off about the ridiculously cheap price of a bottle of whisky on the flight back to Birmingham!

The performance of Bach's B minor Mass that night was electric. There were 2000 in the church (apparently cultural events were the only occasions when more than five people were allowed to be together), and the effect on all of us in the Birmingham contingent of giving this world masterpiece in the composer's own church was overwhelming.

But then came the time to phone in my review back to Birmingham. I had been promised that the parish office would be open and that I could phone from there. Copy all written, I found my way there, to find it was locked! I roamed and roamed, until I found the door of the Parish Priest's own office open, gatecrashed the place, and picked up the phone. It was by now very, very close to the deadline back home.

How I got past the Leipzig operator and through to the Birmingham Post switchboard I'll never remember, but eventually there I was, speaking in rushed tones to one of my favourite copytakers. "This is Christopher Morley, speaking from behind the Iron Curtain, and there's not much time. This is a review of the Birmingham Bach Choir in St Thomas' Church, Leipzig."

"How'm yow spellink LOIPZIG, Chrees?" came back the lovely girl's measured tones. But the review was in the paper next morning and I was eventually able to get to the party downstairs, where apparently many dangerous anti-government speeches had been made, not least by the Parish Priest whose phone had saved my bacon.

It was only a few months after this that the Iron Curtain came down and the Berlin Wall crumbled, and I'm sure the spirit of our Leipzig friends was in the forefront of this momentous event.

Incidentally, I've already mentioned the tiny duty-free shop at Bucharest Airport. That at Leipzig was just the size of a kitchen cabinet. At least you could walk round the one at Tallinn, where there was just enough stuff to have a browse.

Top: A grainy photograph of Zia Rita, my beloved godmother and indeed a second mother to me, wearing my hat, the last time I saw her. Mum, flanked by sisters Lydia and Nina, Sorrento 1981.

Bottom: Godson Simon Lisseter and me playing duets one Christmas night.

Top: Conductor Alexander Anisimov and me, along with Mimi and Musetta, after Rostov Opera's La Boheme at the Grand Theatre, Wolverhampton.
Bottom: Entertaining my Rostov Opera friends at the sadly-missed La Galleria in Birmingham.

Top: Lunch in Tivoli Gardens, Copenhagen, Andrew Jowett third left.

Middle: Late night Tivoli Gardens, Copenhagen, Stephannie Williams second right, me second left. Poppy the cat giving the man she makes out is her master the once-over.

Bottom: The Rock with William Walton's ashes, overlooking my beloved Bay of Naples. Lady Susan Walton as depicted by Andrew Logan at La Mortella, Ischia, Italy. Boneca Vasconcellos and Stephannie Williams on William Walton's funicular at La Mortella.

Top: The critic in his lair. Proposing the toast celebrating Bromsgrove Concerts' 40th anniversary.

Middle: Back to the pavilion after scoring 8 for the Earls staff team. Chez Swedish soprano Elisabeth Söderström.

Bottom: Three generations, John Joubert who taught me and Bruce O'Neil, whom I taught, now Head of Music at the Royal Shakespeare Theatre.

Top: Maureen with my best friend Richard Lisseter and his wife Sue in Half a Sixpence.
Maureen and me, Oklahoma! 1985 (must have been the last night, because I was wearing tails).
Middle: Half a Sixpence, my first show with GEC Amateur Operatic Society.
The 'Confessions' talk at the Elgar Birthplace, Lower Broadheath.
Bottom: Birmingham Festival Choral Society farewell dinner in Amsterdam. I seem to remember the words I wrote to Cwm Rhondda were slightly rude!

Top: On top of the Czech Alps, July 1998. The tiny opera-house in Prague where Mozart's Don Giovanni was premiered.
Middle: Bach and me, outside the composer's St Thomas' Church in Leipzig.
The old city, Tallin, Estonia.
Bottom: Grieg's composing hut, Troldhaugen, Norway. Grieg's House, Troldhaugen.

Beethoven's
Schokoladenseite

Top: The Hermitage Museum and Neva river, St. Petersburg, Russia. Ole Bull, the Paganini or André Rieu of Bergen, Norway.
Middle: Revolting animal abuse in Bruges, Belgium. A cosy chocolate-house in Bonn, Germany.
Bottom: Drawing room of Jean Sibelius, Ainola, Finland. Visiting Sibelius Gardens, Ainola, Finland.

Top: Conducting Haydn's Military Symphony with the CBSO staff orchestra.
On tour with the Birmingham Festival Choral Society, Plovdiv, Bulgaria.
Bottom: Stephen Maddock, Chief Executive of the CBSO, presenting me with my long-service award for my 60th birthday.

The historic Birmingham Festival Choral Society invited me to join them on several trips abroad, the first one being a week in Bulgaria in 1992. The idea was to give concerts (there are agencies which organise all that), but also to make donations to local charities, which was always a big event for the media in whichever country.

We flew to Sofia and then took a very late-night coach to Plovdiv, where we were based for the first part of the week, arriving at our hotel in the wee small hours. But it was not yet bedtime for some of us, as there was a welcoming party waiting to greet us. The grandees had enlisted the services of Krum, a student who spoke excellent English, as an interpreter and a young man who was to become the star of the week.

Plovdiv is a fascinating city. It has the ruins of a Roman amphitheatre as well as the ornate architecture of the Ottoman Empire. It also has wonderful restaurants, from which I chiefly remember dishes involving fried cheese, and all delicious.

There were also dancing bears and I had always been horrified by the idea. But one hot afternoon when some of us were outside our hotel, an old man brought his bear into the grounds, led it to the little pond where it had a good drink and then the two of them curled up and had a sleep on the grass. My thinking began to change, given this evidence of such a trusting bond between them.

The BFCS had twinned up with the local Male Voice Choir, and together we gave a concert in the city's Cathedral. Naturally there was a lot of English music, including Elgar and Stanford, in the BFCS' contributions. But the men of BFCS found it very difficult to concentrate entirely on the music being performed by our Bulgarian friends, as the conductor of the Plovdiv choir was a very young, very attractive with gorgeous tumbling hair, and exceedingly buxom lady. No wonder the Bulgarians performed so enthusiastically for her as she bounced on each beat.

After the concert we returned to our hotel, where a supper was laid out on the terrace for us all – except I had a review to dictate back to Birmingham. While they were all downstairs living it up I was up in the room I shared with Jeremy Patterson, the lovely man who was the much-respected BFCS conductor, desperately trying to make a telephone connection to the Birmingham Post.

The line kept going down and I kept having a shot from my duty-free bottle of whisky. Eventually, after what seemed like a couple of hours (and thank goodness there was a two-hour difference between Bulgaria and the UK), I got through to the copy-desk and there was the voice of Peter Bacon, the wonderful Features Editor, who had taken it upon himself to type out my copy.

I had to shout out every word, the line was so bad. But it worked, and people were able to fax out the printed review to their loved ones in Bulgaria the very next morning. Hungry, I made my way downstairs, where the supper-party was dispersing, but there was Marilyn Seeckts, alto in the choir but also press officer at Birmingham Conservatoire and therefore a close colleague of mine, guarding a supper-plate she'd assembled for me, plus a couple of bottles of beer. The overdose of adrenaline gradually disappeared.

Next morning we set off on the 10-hour coach journey to Varna on the Black Sea. The Male Voice Choir were there to see us off, and I gave what remained of my bottle of whisky to Stefan, a lovely man with whom I had palled up.

The first thing I did when we arrived in Varna was to use the toilet in the hotel room I was again sharing with Jeremy and I broke the handle of the flush. To this day he has never allowed me to forget that and refers to the event in poems to his friends.

Then many of us decided we needed a swim to get rid of the dust of that long journey in a wheezy old coach. I had no bathing-trunks, but found a pair on a seaside stall in a disgusting fluorescent green, donned them in a bathing-hut, and went into the Black Sea.

Which was full of human wastage, honestly. Swimming in such conditions was very little pleasure, so I didn't stay long.

After the very successful concert in Varna, the flight from there back to Sofia was memorable. Krum, who had been enlisted to remain with the BFCS party after his indispensable work on our behalf in Plovdiv, had seen us through all the vicissitudes in Varna too (but not the one where, late one evening, I was looking for somewhere to eat, found a restaurant still open and made gestures to the proprietor, pointing at my mouth and rubbing my stomach; "Yes sir, what can I get you?" he replied in excellent English. I felt very small).

Now Krum was to accompany us back to the capital, and from there return, of course at BFCS' expense to Plovdiv. It was a tiny, ramshackle plane we boarded at Varna Airport and there seemed to be no seat for Krum, and he just vanished into thin air.

The flight took about an hour and the inflight catering was something quite unique. The lone stewardess brought us each a cardboard beaker and a teabag, and then came round with an electric kettle, filling our beakers with boiling water, a trip she had to make many times to get round us all. What a glamorous life it is, being an air hostess.

As we landed at Sofia airport the door leading into the cockpit opened, and who should emerge but Krum, who had obviously scrounged a seat in the flight cabin. But we were all convinced that it was this remarkable young man who had flown the plane and wouldn't have put it past his talents.

My next trip accompanying the Birmingham Festival Choral Society was to Poznan in Poland, and was altogether lower-key, though equally as satisfying artistically. The journey there was hilarious, however.

We travelled by ferry from Felixstowe to Hamburg, which involved an overnight crossing. Some of us stayed up to watch a late-night screening of the then "must-see" film Four Weddings and a Funeral, and I suppose it passed the time.

Arriving in Hamburg the next afternoon, we set off in our coach for Poznan, and seemed to be driving forever, past Berlin, through the eastern part of Germany, and eventually, well after midnight queued at the border to get into Poland.

Once past the frontier we cruised down the motorway, and were intrigued to see bright lights shining at a roadside shop. There on the forecourt were rows and rows of garden gnomes, with people earnestly examining them. Later we learned that Germans are inordinately fond of garden gnomes, and that they are 25% cheaper in Poland, hence the trips over the border. But why so late at night?

One of the highlights of this trip was a morning at the riding-stables in Gniezno, where the military grooms its horses. We were shown round by impeccably-dressed officers, and all the BFCS women swooned (perhaps some of the men, too). And then came the climax, a horse-drawn open-topped cavalcade through the town. I don't know how it happened, but I was seated in the front row of the first carriage with the BFCS publicity officer, waving to the crowds who were lining the streets. I expect the Queen has got pretty well used to this over the years.

On the drive back to Hamburg we stopped off near the border, and guess what present we bought for Mac, our driver? A giant garden gnome.

My next trip with BFCS was to the Czech Republic and this time our coach, with two drivers, took the shuttle through the Channel Tunnel, which was an amazing experience. One of our party suffered terribly with claustrophobia, and Tricia Bradbury, mother of the assistant conductor Anthony Bradbury, did a wonderful job in talking her through the whole half-hour in the darkness, holding her hand and just prattling away. As the train emerged into the French daylight we all burst into applause for both of them.

We arrived in Prague, and I was so thrilled to be able to explore the city where my beloved Mozart had enjoyed such wonderful welcomes. I visited the tiny, tiny theatre where Don Giovanni had been premiered, but I also made a point of visiting the Wenceslaus Square where so many crucial political events had happened in recent decades of my lifetime.

The concert was an afternoon performance in St Nicolas Church in the Old Town Square. The perfume of lilies filled the air, and the music-making was sublime, not least a wonderful performance of Mozart's Laudate Dominum from Pauline Alder.

I rushed back to the hotel, bought a beer in the bar from the charming barmaid, and went up to my room to write and phone in my review. As the evening approached, we all got ready for our evening cruise on the Vltava river (yes, that's got you singing Smetana's great piece in your head, hasn't it). After a pre-cruise drink we assembled on board and sat down for a delicious meal with plenty of wine.

The cruise lasted a couple of hours and after disembarkation some of us went into the Old Town Square for a nightcap or three. It was the little glass of slivovitz at the end which did for me. A group of us took a taxi back to the hotel, and it was only when I was climbing the steps into the foyer that I wondered if I was going to make it, but I did.

Early next morning I woke up, fully clothed, my feet on the pillow where my head should have been and feeling absolutely awful. Breakfast was an hour away, before a three-hour coach drive to Cesky Krumlov, the second and last part of our itinerary.

This was the most monumental hangover in history and I like to joke now that there is a blue plaque on the walls of the Town Hall by the pub where this all happened, and that grown men doff their caps, drop their voices and make the sign of the cross as they pass.

Everyone was very, very kind to me over breakfast and then we boarded the coach for the long journey. Up to now I had sat downstairs at a table with a couple of elderly ladies, one of whom couldn't stop talking and found it hilarious whenever we drove past a sign on the motorway saying "Einfahrt" or "Ausfahrt".

I just couldn't face making polite and incessant conversation, so took myself upstairs, where the awkward squad were ensconced and was greeted with cheers and a huge amount of sympathy. Gradually I returned to the land of the living, drank a revivifying beer at lunchtime when we arrived at our hotel, and by evening time was able to enjoy the supper the local choir put on for us.

After the concert a couple of days later we were invited up to a village in the mountains (this was part of the Alps, after all, on the border with Bavaria), and during the return to our hotel the most immense thunderstorm erupted. I felt as though we were in the middle of Wagner's Die Walkure. A very pleasant couple on the same hotel floor as me had brought a bottle of Tio Pepe on the trip, and that made a very nice end to the evening and my visit to the Czech Republic.

My final trip with BFCS was a couple of years later, beginning in Bruges. What a beautiful city, with all those canals, all that lace, all that chocolate and the TinTin shop.

But what remains a disfiguring memory of Bruges for me was the sight of a man dressed in countryman's gear sitting proudly atop a farm wagon of which every inch, wheels and all, was covered with live creatures in cages slung everywhere, songbirds, chickens, cats, dogs, rabbits and heaven knows what else. All the tourists gawped and took photographs. I was disgusted.

We moved on to Amsterdam, where my highlight was standing in the queue to visit the Anne Frank Museum. What a sobering experience that was.

I felt that these tours were no longer for me. For the members of the choirs involved they were an intensification of emotional bonding (sometimes too much so), and I was not part of that. There was too much of a drink culture, too, and I had learnt not to be part of that either.

But my presence as an individual at international festivals was something very different, and that takes us into the next chapter.

Chapter 11

GLOBETROTTING ALONE

Enjoyable though those tours were, I much preferred being a lone wolf rather than part of a herd and when invitations arrived for me to travel to all sorts of exciting places, then I was happy to accept them, and felt the freedom of being there on my own terms. Any friendships made would be value-added extras, such as that with Michael and Joyce Kennedy.

That happened at La Mortella, the paradisical home of the late Sir William and Lady Susana Walton on the enchanted island of Ischia in the Bay of Naples, my motherland. Susana had created a wonderful garden there (to keep her quiet, Walton used to say, while he was composing), and every year the recently-established Walton Fondazione held a summer school for specially-selected students from British conservatoires to rehearse and perform operas which had been close to the composer's heart.

Stephannie Williams (Steve) was the UK Artistic Director of the William Walton Trust working alongside such luminaries as the Prince of Wales (the Patron), Sir Simon Rattle, Richard Hickox, and other stellar names from the worlds of arts and finance. She and I had worked closely together during her Stratford Festivals, as well as when I interviewed some of the soloists on her client-list, such as the young South Korean pianist Ju Hee Suh, and now she was inviting me to review the performance of the 1996 summer school (the attendance of select groups of British and Italian critics to review was part of the Fondazione's stipulation).

All expenses were paid, including accommodation at the Sporting Hotel Isabella at Lacco Ameno, five-star with its own spa, and we had little bottles of its various muds among the complimentary items in our rooms (along with a bottle of champagne). The critic Michael White was most upset to find he didn't have any mud amongst his tray of goodies and kicked up quite a fuss.

I loved Lacco Ameno, not least for Il Fungo, the tiniest of islets a few metres out of the tiny harbour, looking as though a mushroom had sprouted out of the sea. A ceramic tile of it hangs among many other treasures on one of the walls of my study, to my left as I write.

Among our party, led by Steve, were Michael, nice Roger Watkins of the Evening Standard, who became a very good friend, Conrad Wilson of the Scotsman, Elizabeth Forbes (whose formidable reputation had gone before her, but she was actually very approachable). Suzanne Graham-Dixon, publicist par excellence and her daughter Elizabeth were also there. Already at La Mortella were Michael and Joyce Kennedy, staying at the lodge in the grounds. They were longtime friends of the Waltons.

It was a wonderful long weekend, centring around Susana's generous hospitality at La Mortella and the delicious cooking of her housekeeper, Reale. We had tours of the splendid garden, all the way up to the rock where William Walton's ashes are enshrined, we imbibed Susana's specially-invented Mortella cocktails, we were entertained to limoncello and pizza parties by her neighbours, and so much else besides.

But of course we were chiefly there for the music, and the operas to be performed that year were Rossini's deft little L'Occasione Fa il Ladro, and Walton's own one-acter, The Bear, based on a Chekhov short story. John Gibbons was conducting and the director was Jonathan Miller.

Jonathan and his wife were great company, but unfortunately he and Michael White just didn't hit it off, and a bit of an atmosphere developed. Susana kept everyone in order though.

The performances were given in Walton's music-room and were attended not only by us British critics, but also a contingent of Italian ones, shipped over from Naples for the evening. It was a wonderful evening, though I don't remember any mingling between the two groups of critics. I could have been the Colossus of Rhodes, astride between them both.

At Naples Airport for our return next morning Jonathan kept retreating into the duty-free shop to buy bars of chocolate whenever he saw Michael White approaching! I felt rather subdued as we flew back to England, as it had been such a magical trip. Michael and I sat together on the train from Gatwick to Victoria, and I think we both felt the same. We bumped into each other at a Prom concert in the Royal Albert Hall a few days later, and that was rather nice.

I was invited back to La Mortella the next year, which this time was featuring scenes from Verdi's Falstaff, an opera I have come to adore. There was no Steve this time (she was away on one of the P&O Cruises for which she organised the most amazing Music Festivals), but I think Sue Graham-Dixon and Elizabeth were with us, and we were a slightly different party.

Roger was there, Michael was there and this time we were joined by the esteemed critic Edward Greenfield, friend of the great and the good, who mixed me my first-ever White Lady cocktail, and my old friend and colleague Keith Clarke and his then wife Madeleine. The lovely Kennedys were of course there, and Michael Kennedy and I had a great time, as you will see.

One extra facet to my visit this time was the fact that Sarah Poole, an ex-student of mine at Birmingham Conservatoire, was there as Mistress Quickly, and I did an interview with her for publication back home in the Birmingham Post. That was a strange experience, but it went off very well, and it was lovely to see her again.

This was the week of Princess Diana's funeral and though I was pleased to be out of the country, we still kept up with everything on the television, including the Queen's return to London after much public recrimination and the funeral itself. Susana banned the students from watching the funeral in their quarters (she was fiercely pro-Charles and didn't have a good word to say about Diana). We watched the funeral in our hotel and then went up to La Mortella for lunch, and didn't the feathers fly!

Princess Diana was a great icon for Michael White and he and Susana had a big-time spat over her. Of course Susana came out on top, and the rest of us went very quiet, whilst still enjoying Reale's delicious food.

The opera that year was Verdi's Falstaff (selected scenes) and the original conductor had been replaced by James Lockhart, someone I had long respected, largely because of his association with Welsh National Opera. I can still see him now, conducting rehearsals wearing Bermuda shorts. He was a very quiet, pleasant presence to be around.

Come the performance, the Italian critics arrived. This time the music-room was arranged with a platform running down the centre, culminating in a T-shape at the end where there were a few bits of scenery, including the crucial screen behind which Nanetta and Fenton hid in their embraces (what wonderful, wonderful music Verdi gives them). The Italian mob were on one side of the platform, we Brits on the other (yes, I know I should have been straddling between them).

Michael Kennedy and I were sitting together and we couldn't believe our eyes at what we were seeing and hearing when the Italians started to join in with the arias – purely, I'm sure, to show us that they knew their Verdi. Sadly, there was again no fraternisation between the two camps. I like to think it was because they had the last ferry to catch back to the mainland.

Keith Clarke likes to rib me about the 1960s swimming-trunks I sported whenever we were swimming from the hotel beach, knitted wool with a big white zip up the front. He even published a picture of them (heaven knows how he got that!) in Classical Music magazine, of which he was the editor, and he was convinced that they were the reason a South African heiress staying at the hotel kept cropping up wherever I was. Still, she did introduce me to the writer Gore Vidal over breakfast one morning.

La Mortella was an unforgettable experience, and every time I hear the lapping opening of the Walton Cello Concerto my mind goes back there and to that sunlit sea and the groves in Susana's wonderful garden.

Pesaro

Sue Graham-Dixon arranged some wonderful further invitations for me, including several visits to the annual Rossini Opera Festival held in the composer's birthplace, Pesaro, on the Italian Adriatic coast.

The location was idyllic, the town was enchanting, its centre medieval rather like Tallinn and there was one particular trattoria which remembered me every time I returned, year by year.

There was always a party of UK critics (it was through one of these that I was belatedly invited to join the Critics' Circle, those of us in the "provinces" having no contacts to propose us), we all got on famously and one occasion I did an extended interview for BBC Radio 3. After the opening-night there was always a supper served under the stars, and one year an Italian lady journalist had the temerity to take the remaining seat on this table where we Brits were raucousing. Fortunately I was next to her, able to converse with her in Italian. She had excellent English, too.

Pesaro was lovely, but the trouble is I don't like Rossini! Okay, I conducted to his Thieving Magpie when I was two years old, and I can indeed take the overtures, but after that... So much of his operas seems to be composing by numbers, I'm afraid I find it difficult to get involved (though there will be a Rossini experience in Japan which I will tell you about later), and find myself counting the minutes while the hours drag away. To endure three or four of them on consecutive evenings was like chalking off many centuries in Purgatory.

And then there is all the canary-fancying. Yes, Rossini was writing for star singers, using their prowess in coloratura and tessitura in order to zap their rivals. But where was the music beneath all these torrents of notes? Most of my critic colleagues lapped this up, but I'm afraid I didn't.

Another bugbear was that the performances began at 8pm. Difficult to fit in a supper beforehand, so it meant an impossibly late, bad-for-the-digestion meal long after midnight at whatever desperate dive happened still to be open.

What was good about ROF at Pesaro, though, was the opportunity it offered to see rising young singers subsequently to follow their stellar progress. I particularly remember the mezzo-soprano Daniela Barcellona, so Janet Baker-like in her stage presence and vocal technique, the amazing Peruvian coloratura tenor Juan Diego Florez, and the charismatic mezzo Anna Bonitatibus. There was also the memorable occasion when the great soprano Renata Tebaldi, rival of Maria Callas, was in attendance in the royal box of Pesaro's jewel of an opera-house and we all turned to view this legend waving down at us.

Whatever my discomfort at Pesaro, my attendance there in 2004 provided me with the opportunity for a heartwarming story which is one of the highlights of my life.

2004 marked the 80th birthday of my beloved godmother, Zia Rita, who had come over to Brighton in 1947 to help Mum, her sister, when I was born and who, finding an English husband, settled in Brighton just round the corner from us. She really was a second mother to me (and remained so until her death in 2006), and I loved her to bits, even though she was a bit of a control-freak!

Rita had announced that her greatest dream was to have all her family around her on a beach in Italy and as a birthday present to herself (typically, she decided to be born on leap-year day, just like Rossini, in fact) paid for all her immediate family to accompany her on a summer holiday to Lido di Jesolo, near Venice.

As it happened, the dates coincided with my forthcoming visit to Pesaro and my cousin Rosanna, born in Brighton, but now living in Milan, and I hatched a plot. She told me where Rita and her family (husband Alf, son Paul, son John with his wife Lisa and their three children Michael, Francesca and Sophie) would be staying and I booked myself secretly into the hotel.

Instead of taking the tedious flight from Stansted to Rimini and then by taxi to Pesaro, I flew from Coventry's short-lived but useful Baginton Airport to Venice, where I then took the bus from Marco Polo Airport to Lido di Jesolo and thence to the hotel.

I surreptitiously checked in (it was siesta time, so I knew they would all be asleep). The proprietress, Signora Brenda, knew all about the plot and showed me to my room – which was a suite of rooms with five beds in it! Poor Rosanna was staying in another hotel nearby, as this hotel had been fully booked at the time of asking, and she could so easily have stayed in one of my rooms here.

Having settled in, I contacted Rosanna and we arranged to meet for a drink in the hotel bar prior to the time of the evening meal, and before Rita and family would be descending. Which is what we did, tucked away invisibly behind a pillar.

The lift descended and Rosanna went to greet her mother, telling her, "oh, there's someone here I'd like you to meet." Grudgingly making her way round the pillar, Rita saw me, and it was wonderful!

She was overjoyed to see me, told me off for mispronouncing the "s" in Pesaro (it should be more like a half-"zed" sound), and then we all went into the dining-room for supper. There was an individual table assigned to the Godden family and now with an extra place for me.

"But who is he?" asked John's kids, who were too young to remember me and their father explained. Pasta has never tasted better, and later that evening we all went out for a passeggiata along the Lido's boulevard, and stopped for a delicious granita at one of the gelaterie.

Arriving back at the hotel, John and family went to bed, but the rest of us stayed on the terrace for a nightcap and I introduced Zia Rita to Montenegro, a tasty amaro I myself had been introduced to by a head waiter in Venice.

Next morning we went down to the beach, had lunch, and then I was about to set off to catch the train from Mestre (on the mainland, just before you cross into Venice) when the barman appeared. I had forgotten to settle the late-night drinks bill!

In Pesaro I developed a bit of a cold, and was so relieved to get back to Jesolo to be with my nearest and dearest again, and immediately felt much better. We had another lovely time on the beach, a meal in the hotel and then it was off back to England for me, after such a wonderful family experience. I loved my Zia Rita very much, as she did me, and I was so glad we both had this memory to treasure.

Palermo

Sue Graham-Dixon also arranged for me to be present at the re-opening of the Teatro Massimo in Palermo after a Mafia-induced darkness lasting many years. The opera selected was Schoenberg's epic Moses und Aron, and it was a fabulous production.

This was my first visit to Sicily, apart from a touchdown at Palermo airport on a cheapo flight back from Naples to Luton in 1979 and I really enjoyed the experience, especially eating the arancini rice-balls for the first time.

I had a haircut in one of the backstreets, I think in Via Berlioz (Hector would have loved that, knowing what I think of most of his music!), and I had a wonderful time exploring this fascinating city.

But the most memorable experience was the actual hotel in which I was staying, the Grand Hotel e delle Palme. This really was a grand hotel and I felt very much at home there (though I did have a fall in the slippery shower, complained down at reception, and did they give me a bottle of champagne to placate me? – no, just a dimpled mat which should have been there in the first place).

The fantastic thing was that this was the hotel where Wagner had stayed as he was working on the completion of his final opera, Parsifal. In the foyer was a glass case displaying the piano-stool which he had used (when I say in my talks version of "Confessions" that I have seen Wagner's stool in a glass case this always causes great hilarity for some reason), but I had something more intimate to treasure.

My bedroom was right next door to Wagner's own! That had now been turned into a little conference-room, but I stole my way in there in order to soak up the atmosphere, and that has stayed with me ever since.

I was invited back to Palermo for a production of Berg's Lulu, all full of mirrors as I seem to recall. The two presentations I saw at this magnificent opera-house were of two of the 20th-century's most problematic operas, and they were proudly done. It would have been so easy to offer Verdi or Puccini in the circumstances (or, most obviously of all, Cavalleria Rusticana – what a fabulous little opera that is! – and Pagliacci), but no. Schoenberg and Berg set out the stall of what the Teatro Massimo was determined to achieve, and it did so triumphantly.

Nordic Festivals

During the time of Steve Williams' Stratford Festivals, Birmingham European Airways decided to name one of its aircraft "Stratford" and I was invited, along with a few others, to be present on its inaugural flight from Birmingham to Copenhagen. Ted Lloyd, the then Mayor of Stratford, was our overwhelmingly ebullient host.

We stayed in the palatial Hotel d'Angleterre and next morning had a working breakfast with one of Copenhagen's top council officials in the huge Town Hall, walking past two large statues on a column outside the wonderful Tivoli Gardens, each of the men poised to play a Lur, an impressive-looking trumpet-like instrument. You never hear the sounds of this instrument, as legend has it that a fanfare will only be played if ever a virgin walks past. The silence is deafening.

I still treasure the tie I was given on that occasion. Later that day, before our flight back to Birmingham, we were taken by coach to Helsingor, with its Renaissance castle built on the site of Hamlet's Elsinore, and just a stone's throw across the straits to Sweden.

It was a beautiful afternoon, and the drive up the coastline was fascinating, with all the little jetties and summerhouses evoking Tove Jansson's delightful *The Summer Book*. We arrived at the castle.

And as we did so, right on cue, an enormous storm erupted. The only thing missing from the thunder and lightning was the ghost of Hamlet's father appearing on the ramparts. And then, as we were about to return to Copenhagen, the storm petered out and we drove back through the ruined ancient settlement of Gurre, I was reminded of Schoenberg's fantastic and epic Gurrelieder.

This was only my first encounter with Denmark and with Scandinavia in general and I was to make many visits to the Baltic countries, not only with the CBSO (as already described), but also through the vibrant festivals organised by Steve Williams.

She had brought many Scandinavian artists over to Stratford for her Festivals, as a result of which she was invited to organise a Nordic Young Artists' Festival in London. And as a result of that, arts organisations in Sweden and Denmark begged her to arrange major festivals in this country and Birmingham, with its wonderful Symphony Hall, was the obvious place in which to locate them.

Sounds of Sweden came first and during the preceding winter an advance party consisting of Roger Watkins, Martin Denny (one of the staff on Steve's Stephannie Williams Artists agency) and me were invited over to snowy Stockholm, where we were looked after by the genial and gargantuan Hugo Ramsten.

Hugo and his wife, the English soprano Rosemary Hardy, whom I'd admired in many contemporary music performances, entertained us to an elk dinner in one of Stockholm's most exclusive restaurants. He also took us to the jewel of a baroque opera-house at Drottningholm, just by the summer Royal Palace, which was specially opened up at my request so that I could see all the wonderful stage-machinery, not least the amazing capstan.

And then, again at my request, he arranged for the wonderful soprano Elisabeth Söderström to entertain us to tea at her family home. This was a real family home, with her grandchildren's toys all over the place, and she so comfortably domesticated there. She was one of my idols, having seen her as tormented Janacek heroines in Welsh National Opera productions, and having enjoyed her recordings with WNO under Richard Armstrong of Britten's song-cycles "Our Hunting Fathers" and "Les Illuminations", as well as singing soprano solo in the CBSO/Rattle recording of Britten's War Requiem. Her command of a panoply of languages was amazing.

This trip coincided with the demonstrations against the proposed Newbury bypass in Berkshire and it was incessantly on the BBC TV channel we were able to access. Chief mischief-maker was a young lad called Swampy and that was what Roger and I immediately rechristened Martin Denny! He loved it.

Sounds of Sweden in Birmingham was a huge success, and I particularly enjoyed the opening concert in Symphony Hall. The compering was shared between Elisabeth Söderström and Ulrika Jonsson, who was big news at the time as a television personality (I also saw her performing in the fabulous musical The Pajama Game at Birmingham Repertory Theatre, a show I had conducted myself, and she was great, whatever prejudiced reviewers who know less about musicals than I do wrote).

Star of this opening evening was the great Swedish tenor Nicolai Gedda, who had been a great hero of mine ever since I bought his recording of La Boheme with Mirella Freni, Thomas Schippers conducting, for my parents' 20th wedding anniversary in 1966.

Sounds of Sweden was a triumph, and as a result of my coverage of the festival I was invited back to Stockholm the next summer for Nordic Music Days, an intense few days when composers from Denmark, Finland, Iceland, Norway and Sweden set out their stalls, each country rotating as host.

I remember it being incredibly hot, and also depressing. We moan about the lack of support given to creative artists in this country, but in Scandinavia (as in Germany) the generosity of support means the creators are not actually hungry, and can indulge themselves profitably to their hearts' content with little thought of communication to the general public.

I used to love contemporary music, in fact I was a passionate champion of it and used to teach it at Birmingham Conservatoire, but now I despair when I attend a concert filled with navel-gazing, and can immediately tell the difference between the offerings of a British composer struggling in this country and a British composer who has a sinecure working in some cosy academy in Germany. No names, no pack-drill.

Over those well-filled few Nordic Music Days I remember only four works I was pleased to have heard, and the best of those came from an American composer living in Iceland!

Such was the success of Sounds of Sweden that Steve Williams was now approached by Denmark to promote something even better for them, and Discover Denmark was the amazing result, a month-long cornucopia of events presented largely in Birmingham's Symphony Hall and Town Hall.

A select party of us was flown over to Copenhagen for a spectacular press launch, which included a concert in the hall of the wonderful Tivoli Gardens and a lunch next day in the fabulous, Disneyland-like galleon moored there.

Apparently there was a huge midwives' conference (not a conference for huge midwives, you understand) going on in Copenhagen at the time, so there were no hotel rooms available. So we were bussed over the impressive new Oresund bridge to Malmo in Sweden to overnight there. As we attempted to open the sliding doors into the hotel we had to be careful not to disturb a little hedgehog that was curled up asleep between the two doors. Unlike the hedgehog, some of us stayed up talking until 4 o'clock in the morning.

There was also a press briefing in one of the smaller halls at the International Convention Centre in Birmingham, where the London contingent arrived well-lubricated (see *Beyond the Notes*, Brewin Books), and which set everything fair for the opening of Discover Denmark.

Before that, though, I was invited to return to Copenhagen to get a taste of the musical scene there and I had a wonderful time in that fascinating city, not least making the impressive train trip to the neighbouring island of Funen, where I was given a tour of Nielsen's childhood home, and where I toured the Birthplace Museum of Hans Christian Andersen in Odense. One of the rooms there is a library housing every edition in existence of the author's writing, and there, on one of the shelves was the ancient Victorian translation into English of his fairy-stories from which my beloved grandmother used to read to me in front of the fire (where we used to look for pictures) when I was really very, very tiny.

The Discover Denmark festival itself was a huge success, with concerts to review almost every day over a whole month. It was exhausting but very rewarding and a huge triumph for Steve Williams, which was nothing unusual, given the Midas touch she possessed.

Drottningholm

I had read about this tiny quarter-of-a-millennium old opera-house preserved in aspic just outside Stockholm, and was thrilled when it had been opened up especially for me during that winter visit pre-Sounds of Sweden.

I was even more thrilled when I received an invitation to review there. I think that was partly because the new music director there, Mark Tatlow, was a Wolverhampton lad (actually son of a builders' merchant), and therefore there would be much Midland interest in this appointment; whatever, for several years I was a regular guest at this most beautiful venue.

The loveliest approach to Drottningholm was on the boat leaving the Stockholm quayside very early in the evening, with a restaurant serving three-course suppers as we sailed up the archipelago past countless tiny islands, most with their little houses.

The theatre was a little jewel (a description so often overused, including by me). As I entered it for the first time I was hit by the heat within the auditorium (all wood), and saw there was an empty seat in the centre, a few rows from the stage. That's mine, I thought, until I realised they were the two thrones occupied by the King and Queen.

There were only two loos in the place, which made the intervals difficult. The grounds outside were beautiful, with a lake just below the theatre which geese had made their own, and heaven help anyone who came near. I seem to remember the interval wine wasn't very good, and it was always a coach-ride back to Stockholm city centre.

I saw some wonderful productions at Drottningholm, including operas by Monteverdi, Mozart and Haydn (Pesaro and tedious Rossini, eat your heart out). The stage-effects were fascinating, with cutouts of waves going up and down for seascapes, flats suddenly swivelling (thanks to the massive capstan down below the stage), and touchingly elemental thunder and lightning effects. The whole impression was of a grown-up version of a child's toy theatre.

It was always a great experience being there, but there was an oddity. My invitations always paid for the travel, but never for the accommodation. Was I expected to sleep on the floor at the airport? So I booked myself into hotels on the internet and was always very comfortable, except for the fact that, depending upon how much city tax they were paying, the licensing hours were accordingly restricted. I became unusually grumpy when I returned at 10pm one Sunday night and couldn't get a beer. And the last hotel I booked myself into turned out to be a temperance hotel, so I was not a happy bunny.

But I loved my Drottningholm years, and the good relationship I forged with Mark Tatlow. The last time we met was when I interviewed him over breakfast in my temperance hotel, but mind you, that hotel introduced me to a lovely breakfast dish of chopped tomatoes and sweetcorn. That was worth going dry for.

There was a thread which was ever-present in all my visits to Drottningholm. At the very end of Gamlastan, which runs all the way through the centre of Stockholm, there was a bookshop and there in the window was an enticing English-language Billy Bunter compendium, priced absurdly cheaply. I've always loved Billy Bunter, my brother Aldo even more so (he once wrote a fan letter to Gerald Campion, who played the Fat Owl of the Remove in the BBC television series in the 1950s and 60s, and was thrilled to receive a reply), and I wanted it.

But the shop was shut. As it was every time I returned to Stockholm, with that book still in the window. I asked the postman who happened to be passing once when I was there, and he couldn't tell me what their opening hours were. I found the shop's website and emailed them. No reply.

I don't think I was meant to have the book. I wonder if it's still there in the window.

Bergen

Another wonderful Scandinavian venue I visited several times was Bergen, nestling amid the Norwegian fjords, and in many ways somewhat similar to Copenhagen in its gracious squares, its ancient wooden buildings, and its general relationship with the sea. I love both places, much in the way I love Venice (though the architecture and atmosphere there are of course totally different). I've only now realised, I've never reviewed in Venice.

My first trip to Bergen was in the winter, and I was invited there by the Bergen Philharmonic Orchestra, who were shortly to visit Symphony Hall here in Birmingham. My journey there was quite fraught, as the plane from Birmingham had a delayed landing in Amsterdam and I had to rush through the nightmarish Schiphol Airport to catch the connecting flight to Bergen. My hold-luggage didn't make it (I now try just to travel with cabin-luggage), but turned up later that evening at the Nelson Hotel where I'd been booked in (at Bergen's expense, Drottningholm take note). Full marks to KLM Airlines.

The Bergen Phil were performing Grieg's rarely-heard sole attempt at opera, Olav Trygvason, in their magnificent Grieghalle home. I was mightily impressed both with the venue and the quality of the orchestra, which has remained one of my favourite ensembles, partly because of the excellence of their conductors I have known and worked with (Andrew Litton and Edward Gardner).

Bergen is so rewarding to explore. As well as Grieg, it has another great son, the writer Ludvig Holberg, almost Norway's equivalent of Shakespeare and Moliere. He is, of course, commemorated in Grieg's nostalgic Holberg Suite (what a great piece!), and his play Maskarade was transformed into an opera by Carl Nielsen and is now Denmark's national opera; I attended a performance on one of my visits to Copenhagen.

Overlooking Bergen's splendid harbour is a statue of Holberg gazing out to sea. And the gulls like to use his head as a perching place while they do the same thing.

But Norwegian publishers have missed a trick. I looked everywhere for a bilingual edition of Holberg's works, such as the Shakespeare plays I have in English on one page, in Italian on the opposite one, but apparently one doesn't exist. Bad marketing.

Grieg is, of course and rightly, universally known and loved and the summer home he had built at Troldhaugen, up in the hills just outside the city, is a haven of tranquility. It is perched on the edge of a lake with water so clear you can see the fish cavorting, and Grieg's ashes, along with those of his wife Nina are enshrined in the cliffside there (memories of William and Susana Walton's rock at La Mortella).

During the winter months the house was closed, but Erling Dahl, the charming curator, opened it up for me and gave me a tour. It was magical to be in the rooms where the Griegs had lived their everyday lives, to see Grieg's piano (and Erling gave me a CD of transfers of the composer playing his own music on this very piano, including of course Wedding Day at Troldhaugen), and just to soak up the atmosphere.

I was also allowed into Grieg's composing hut next door, with its little fire, its piano-stool bolstered by volumes of Beethoven to raise the little man up to a playable height and its fantastic views across the lake.

Grieg was indeed a tiny man, and there is a lifesize statue just outside. Erling took a photograph of six-foot me embracing the genius. I wonder how many people have had the same picture taken? And why was it okay for me to do that, when I get so angry at the sight of grinning tourists posing alongside the Little Mermaid in Copenhagen?

I was reluctant to leave Troldhaugen, but I was indeed to return, on my next visit which was in the spring, for the Bergen Festival. This was a vibrant event, with a lively press launch on the opening morning, which I seem to remember was held in the open air, on the terrace of an hotel. I was there with the Daily Telegraph and BBC Radio 3 critic Ivan Hewett, and we got on very well.

My own hotel was in the little square dominated by the statue of the violinist Ole Bull, Norway's answer to Paganini, and an international superstar in his own right, making a fortune as the result of tours to the United States. The Andre Rieu of his day, perhaps.

In the glorious spring weather I explored again this lovely city. I bought a dish of crab and prawns in the vibrant quayside market, and after enjoying that I took the nearby cable-car trip up the mountainside to the most fantastic lunar-like landscape at the top, just a few minutes away (sorry, I must stop to tell you I am listening as I write to my recording of the CBSO playing Grieg's Symphonic Dances, Sakari Oramo conducting; the second one is just so painfully gorgeous).

The views from there, down to Bergen and across the harbour to the open sea, are breathtaking and everywhere there are little lakes, just like the tarns at the top of the fells in our own Lake District.

Just beyond the open-air market is the row of merchants' houses from the time centuries ago when Bergen was part of the Hanseatic league of trading ports. One of these is a museum and it was fascinating to explore. I was struck by how dark it was inside, even in bright daylight, and of course it was all wood in construction. There have been several disastrous fires down the centuries.

On our last day in Bergen, Ivan and I attended a lunchtime recital in the intimate little concert-hall at Troldhaugen, which falls down towards the lake, clearly visible through the window which is the whole expanse of the stage end of the auditorium and which has a grass-covered roof, so that it merges imperceptibly with the landscape.

Immediately the concert ended a taxi arrived to speed us to the airport, and that was my second farewell to Bergen, but happily not my last.

The Bergen Philharmonic were planning another trip to Birmingham, under their recently-appointed new principal conductor Edward Gardner, and I had no hesitation in jumping at their invitation to hear them again in their home base before their visit here. I knew Ed well as he had been a popular principal guest conductor of the CBSO (and I had probably heard him as a young chorister at Gloucester Cathedral). He was in the process of making an important series of recordings for Chandos of the Mendelssohn and Schubert symphonies with the CBSO in Birmingham Town Hall. I needed no prompting to take this opportunity to catch up with him and his wonderful new orchestra again.

This was a 24-hour trip in December and Bergen was at its notorious wettest. No matter, it was great to be back again. My host was Henning, the BPO's press officer, a lovely, genial man. I was joined on the trip by Hugh Canning of the Sunday Times and Opera magazine. We had an amazing meal of mussels in a packed, lively restaurant before the concert, which was Haydn's great oratorio The Creation.

It was a fantastic performance and there was a lovely reception afterwards for a select group of guests, including the soloists, some of whom I knew from concerts in England, Ed Gardner, of course, Hugh and me. I remember the food was delicious and the champagne went down well.

I'm not a night owl these days, so I left fairly early on and walked back to the nearby hotel. But I took myself up to the bar at the very top of this huge building, where I could observe this sparkling city gradually putting itself to bed, whilst I drank a nightcap.

Next morning I had an interview with Ed Gardner in his office at the Grieghalle, and we seemed to spend most of the time talking about cricket, and how he had once wangled a trip to Australia to see England play test matches there!

Henning took Hugh and me for lunch at an amazing restaurant within a spectacular fish market mall on the harbour side where the daily catch was landed, and then it was time to leave.

Moldova and Romania

Down at the other end of Europe, I had a couple of extraordinary invitations to the Balkans, the first of them being to a tiny country I had scarcely heard of and which might make many readers scurry to an atlas.

Moldova came into existence after the fall of the Iron Curtain. I couldn't begin to explain the politics of how it happened, but geographically it is a little chunk of southeastern Romania. It's almost on the Black Sea, but not quite. I went there at the generous invitation of Ellen Kent.

Ellen Kent ran a tremendous opera and ballet enterprise, scouring the old eastern bloc countries for companies which would give their eye teeth to be engaged for a lucrative tour performing in the United Kingdom. The schedules were gruelling, covering the length and breadth of the country, staying sometimes in the same venue for a number of performances, but otherwise uprooting every day to pop up somewhere else.

However demanding these tours were, they were welcomed by the artists, who were able to earn a lot of money which they then spent on items not easily available back home. Apparently instrument vans would be filled with white goods, and instrument cases crammed with personal goodies (where the instruments themselves went, I wouldn't know). It also gave the performers the chance to establish their own little touring "families", but we won't investigate that any further.

Ellen was planning to bring the Chisinau National Opera over to the UK, and she invited a small group of critics and theatre managers from places where the company would be performing to go over to Moldova for the weekend, where the company would be presenting its wares.

We assembled at Charles de Gaulle Airport in Paris, ready to take the flight on to Chisinau, the capital of Moldova. On arrival in that country we were ushered into an important-looking office and issued with our visas, splendid-looking things stuck into our passports. It emerged that we were the only Brits in Moldova that weekend, which is a bit of a scary thought.

Our hotel was magnificent, and certainly the finest in the country. There were leather sofas outside the lifts on every floor, and in each of our rooms was a bottle of Moldovan sparkling wine and a bottle of Moldovan red wine. It was obvious we were going to be treated like visiting royalty, and we were.

After dinner, where we fraternised with a charming wedding-party probably spending their life-savings on an evening which we just pamperedly took in our stride, we took the lift back up to our floor, and sat on the sofas discussing our evening. There were two very attractive ladies on one of the sofas, with elaborate make-up and hairstyles, and the photographer in our party couldn't resist taking pictures of them as they tittered behind their hands.

They should have charged him for those photos, as they were hookers, waiting for thick-walleted clients in this most expensive of hotels. Next morning, as we went down for breakfast, there were their pimps, waiting for them in the foyer, ready to take them and their takings home. So very, very sad.

After breakfast we went out to explore, and were immediately struck by the poverty contrasting with what we were experiencing. There were tiny little tables set up in the streets, selling all kinds of tat which no-one could possibly want to buy, and there was a general atmosphere of needy stoicism in a very rundown city.

Later that morning we had a meeting with the Minister of Culture, a charming man whom I seem to remember had an interest in contemporary music, and then we began a round of performances which were actually embarrassing in the lavish hospitality bestowed upon us.

We were sat in what might have been the Royal (or Stalin's) Box in an empty theatre, while a deft Marriage of Figaro (with an excellent Cherubino) unfolded before us. On the shelf in front of our seats were boxes of chocolates and bottles of brandy and sparkling wine. Opera-going was never like this in Birmingham.

I can't remember what filled the rest of the evening, but next morning we appeared for breakfast before another important meeting, and one of our party was missing. He was a particularly hard-drinking, overweight bon viveur and as our departure time for the meeting neared, we began to get worried.

Another chap and I went up to his room and the chambermaid let us in immediately (bad security lapse?). We entered, wondering whether we'd find him dead and there he was, fast asleep and actually dead to the world. We roused him, told him what time it was, and went back to the rest of our party. And he appeared, on the dot of departure time! I see him now every year at Longborough and he has lost a lot of weight, is far more abstemious, and now has a strong woman in control of him.

We were given a tour of the most amazing wine-cellar which ran for kilometres underground, and we needed a little buggy to transport us around it. The Nazis had pillaged it during World War II, but there were still riches galore there. They like to tell everyone that Yuri Gagarin, the first cosmonaut to orbit the earth, was once entombed in there for two days, and emerged very happy.

That afternoon we were the guests at another operatic presentation, with again the panoply of goodies, but for some reason everything was running late and Ellen Kent brought matters to a close. The performers were bitterly disappointed, as they had gone to so much trouble and expense to sell themselves to us, and a bit of an atmosphere developed. There was going to be more of that.

In the evening we attended a public performance by the ballet company of Tchaikovsky's Nutcracker (or was it Swan Lake?). Beforehand, though, there was a reception mounted by Moldovan TV, and I was nominated to be our representative to be interviewed for live broadcast. It all went very well, and the charming interviewer had wonderful English. She sat next to me during the first act, texting her husband the whole time, and left at the interval.

There were so many other events, but on the final afternoon the men in our party were able to escape to a nearby park for a quiet beer, away from all the politics and shenanigans. We sat at a table, and a nice little waitress came out to take our orders. The six of us each asked for a beer.

She brought the beers and the bill, which was something ridiculous, the equivalent of two US dollars. I had brought dollars and said I would pay. I gave her a five-dollar bill and indicated she should keep the change. I can still see her now, running from shop to shop around the park, showing her friends this five-dollar bill which was now hers. We don't know we're born.

This was the final evening of the trip and it ended on a sour note. After the final performance, the management of Chisinau National Opera invited us for a farewell meal, and we were taken to a cosy restaurant nearby. There was a little party going on in a different part of the room, either a birthday or a wedding, and a small instrumental group was playing nice background music for them.

We Brits were at the bottom of the long table allocated to our party, all the political bigwigs at the top. The meal was lovely, but suddenly we realised that the music had stopped, and the people in the other party were looking really miffed. It turned out that Ellen Kent had felt a headache coming on, and ordered that the music be stopped. And such was her power and influence in providing work for Chisinau National Opera that the music was indeed stopped.

For me and all the others it was an uncomfortable end to what had been a fascinating trip.

Some years later I was invited to the biennial Enescu Festival in Bucharest, celebrating Romania's greatest musician, not only as a composer, but also as a conductor and violinist (his recording of the Bach Double Violin Concerto with Yehudi Menuhin is legendary).

The concert on my first evening was given by the Vienna Philharmonic Orchestra conducted by Franz Welser-Most (everyone in the music profession knows that his nickname is Frankly Worst-than-Most), and it was dull, dull, dull. Next night the orchestra was the Royal Liverpool Philharmonic under Vasily Petrenko, and the result could not have been more different, with such a galvanising effect on the audience.

Talking of the audience, they and the stewards didn't bother what time they rolled into the concert, and where they sat. If they didn't like their allocated seats, they wandered around – during the music – until they found one they preferred. I was reminded of my visit to the New York City Ballet in the Lincoln Center (can I really allow myself to spell it like that?), when as soon as the performance started (and it was the magically quiet opening of Samuel Barber's Violin Concerto) they would all spill out of their seats to ensconce themselves at the front of the gallery.

What was amazing was that not only did the Enescu Festival pay for my flights and accommodation, they also gave me a daily emolument for living expenses, just in the same way as orchestral players are treated. I made my contribution by agreeing to be interviewed live on Romanian radio as I emerged from one of the concerts.

I was booked into an elegant fin-de-siecle art nouveau hotel. My bedroom was spectacularly gracious, and the dining-rooms were intriguingly varied. The first night I ate in the silver-service restaurant, with a pianist tinkling away onstage, the second night I ate down in the bistro (where they had Worcestershire Sauce available, something I hadn't been able to get at the Radnorshire Arms in Presteigne, in the next county to Worcestershire), and on the third night I decided to order my late supper on the hotel's wonderful terrace overlooking Bucharest.

You wouldn't think a croque monsieur would take an hour and a half to cook, but it did. I went to enquire several times, but apparently there had been a powercut in the kitchen, and then later World War III between the kitchen staff. Eventually the delicious dish did appear, plus a complimentary bottle of wine, which saw me through the last couple of days.

A few other invitations

I don't remember how this invitation came about, but I had a weekend in Ghent in order to review a Flanders Opera production of Mozart's La Clemenza di Tito (wonderful score, dire drama – my opinion of the piece, not of that particular production).

There was a generous welcome pack waiting for me at my hotel, a toughened plastic document case containing all kinds of goodies, including a bottle of gin. I ate the best steak I'd ever eaten up to that time (I suspect it was horsemeat and nowadays my teeth can only cope with the wonderful minute steaks at Cafe Rouge and the sadly defunct Carluccio's), I had mussels and frites (the husband and wife on the next table were having a spectacular "domestic"), and I had a tour of the Castle of the Counts, with its gruesome torture chamber and original guillotine.

After the opera was over (nothing to write home about, though of course I had to), I took the train to Brussels Airport, where, browsing the bookshop, I seized upon the French translation of Kitty Kelley's *The Royal Family*, a book which at that time was banned in England (and it did say some juicy things about the Queen Mother and Princess Margaret). I so hoped I would be intercepted by the Customs on my landing at Birmingham, and the book being seized, but I was disappointed.

There were also visits to Dortmund in the industrial area of northwest Germany with the CBSO, where I had a tour of a huge coalmining area which had been transformed into an arts complex (and was given a natty shoulder-bag as a keepsake), and to Stuttgart for their Bach Festival, where I was looked after royally, and where every bar served draught wine instead of draught beer – and it was very, very good, thanks to the vine-planting of my Roman ancestors.

I was also the guest on a couple of occasions at the Herrenchiemsee Festival, centring on the last Royal palace built by King Ludwig II of Bavaria, on an island in the middle of an idyllic lake surrounded by the Bavarian Alps. Ludwig wanted to emulate the Versailles of Louis XIV, and created his own Hall of Mirrors, where the main concerts were held. The effect of the 52 chandeliers reflected in those mirrors across the back wall and down the side wall (the other side were windows looking down onto the magnificent lake) was awesome.

To be frank, the concerts were not top-of-the-range, though I do remember a performance of Schumann's Rhenish Symphony, which I have loved since my late teens. What I did take away with me, though, was a taste for the aperitif Aperol, which I had encountered during one of the intervals, and which didn't stick in my craw (wherever that is) even though I had had to pay for it myself.

But there was one German venue which was a constant in my life over very many years, and which more than deserves a section of its own.

Bonn

One day a press release popped into my email inbox detailing the forthcoming Beethovenfest in Bonn, early in the coming autumn. It was a month-long festival of goodies (not all Beethoven, of course), with some of the Beethoven works duplicated by different visiting performers. It looked irresistible, and I registered my interest.

Back came an invitation for a three-day stay, transport and accommodation at the Festival's expense, and which three days would I like to choose?

I was due to go to Berlin to interview Lothar Zagroszek, who was soon to conduct his Konzerthausorchester Berlin at Symphony Hall, so I thought that trip could then be extended to take in Bonn.

It was a thrill to be in Berlin, though there was scarcely time to explore anything, and Zagroszek was a charming interviewee. That evening I attended a concert from his orchestra in the Konzerthaus, which has the most gracious auditorium, all blue and white decor and with separate little throne-like seats for the audience.

Next morning I flew on to Cologne/Bonn airport, where I was met by an enthusiastic young intern music student and driven to Bonn and installed in my hotel. It was a very comfortable establishment, with a terrace bar and cosy restaurant, but I came to realise I was currently in the Festival's third division of hotels, as over the years I was gradually upgraded until, after three years, I was in the most paradisical hotel possible, where I was accommodated for every visit afterwards.

That first visit was a time for establishing myself, and I formed a warm working relationship with the Press Officer, Silke Neubarth. She had a passion for the band Depeche Mode for some reason, and followed them around Europe.

It was a heady weekend, with a round of concerts, a visit to Beethoven's birthplace, which, though crowded with tourists on the museum floors of the house, found me all alone in the tiny room at the very top of the house where the composer was born. That was more than magical.

Next door but one was Im Stiefel, a welcoming, ancient pub, all carved wood and with delicious local food and well-kept beer. Of course I had my lunch there, and they told me Beethoven used to drink there every night. Yeah, right. Queen Elizabeth I never slept there either. But I used the story when I wrote about this amazing visit in my subsequent roundup for the Birmingham Post.

On this first visit I asked to be taken to the asylum in the Endenich suburb of Bonn where Schumann had been incarcerated for the last two years of his life, after his suicide attempt by jumping into the Rhine, pockets laden with stones, from a bridge in Dusseldorf. It is now a dedicated library and recital hall (so heartbreaking to hear Schumann's own music performed there in the house where he died), but also preserves the room which was Schumann's.

I looked through the little window in the door through which Clara Schumann and Brahms, Clara holding Schumann's new baby son, peeped in at the poor man. His doctors forbade any kind of contact between them, even visual, fearing an outburst of Schumann's mental instability. I also walked around the garden in which he was permitted to exercise. You should know that Schumann is a composer very close to my heart for the works he gave us in every genre, and for his warmly human life which ended so tragically.

The only elephant in the room of the Beethovenfest, year after year, was the ghastliness of the Beethovenhalle concerthall. The approach to it walking along the banks of the Rhine was beautiful, but the arrival was disappointing. The building is typically 1950s, functional, inelegant, the foyer is vast in a desire to impress, and the auditorium is the same. Attempts have been made to create an acceptable acoustic, but with little success.

For years the Beethovenfest had been going on at the city authorities wish to give Beethoven's birthplace a concert-hall worthy of his name, but the appeal had come up against all kinds of obstacles. I became involved in these machinations, at first politely at a distance, but then, during the interval of one of my subsequent visits, I was buttonholed by a very vociferous party who wanted me to do all I could.

What could I do? Nothing. I like to think I have some influence in Birmingham, but as a visiting critic in a foreign city? No influence at all. Enough of all of that; Bonn's concert-hall problems go on.

Invitations followed year after year (by this time I was flying from Birmingham to Dusseldorf and then an absorbing train-ride, passing through Cologne, to Bonn itself), and in the third year I was installed in the Konigshof Hotel on the banks of the Rhine, in a room with a balcony overlooking the river. It was just a short walk into the old city and a short walk up to the Beethovenhalle. Breakfasts (with Sekt, the German version of Prosecco) were on the terrace with views across the Rhine of the Siebengebirge, the seven-peaked range of hills which were always to remain in Beethoven's memory when he moved to Vienna, and all the boat traffic making its slow way past on that majestic river.

One time I joined a cruise boat going upriver from Cologne to somewhere much further south, and after an hour disembarked at Konigswinter, where there was a funicular taking us up to the castle of Drachenfels.

The views from here up and down the Rhine were amazing, and I felt that Wagner was very close. Had this location been the inspiration for his Ring cycle? The river was so spectacular here, and I could imagine the Hall of the Gibichungs located nearby, from which poor tormented Brunnhilde walks cackling down to the riverbank in the middle of the night just before the denouement of Gotterdammerung.

And the name Drachenfels itself: it means "dragon mountain". As I walked back down from the ruined castle at the top I saw lizards swarming up the walls. Were these the inspiration for Fafner, the dragon slain by Siegfried?

I made sure I was in Bonn whenever the CBSO was invited. They came at first for one-off performances, but in 2014 were there to give a complete cycle of Beethoven symphonies conducted by the charismatic Andris Nelsons, joined of course for the Ninth Symphony by the CBSO Chorus. This was quite an occasion, and I felt so proud to be part of it. People had come from all over Germany to hear it, and I had some lovely conversations.

I think it was that year as well when the Beethovenfest decided it would replicate the Last Night of the Proms which was going on simultaneously in London's Royal Albert Hall. I was one of a small English contingent singing Land of Hope and Glory (jingoistic claptrap I had resolutely set my face against since last singing it at the Last Night in 1966, Sir Malcolm Sargent's last-ever), standing there waving my passport in the Beethovenhalle. Thank goodness no-one I knew was there in Bonn to see me.

The CBSO's Beethoven cycle was an undoubted highlight and a huge success, but a personal highlight for me was when Nike Wagner was appointed artistic director of the Beethovenfest.

Meeting her came very close to my encounter with Leonard Bernstein in Venice all those years ago in 1968. Here I was, one-to-one with the great-grand-daughter of Richard Wagner, and great-great-grand-daughter of Franz Liszt, not just on one occasion but for three interviews.

Nike is strikingly beautiful, and it's no surprise that she used to be a dancer. In profile she resembles so much her great-great-grandfather Franz, via his daughter Cosima, who married Wagner after an illicit liaison. During our conversations there were hints of the political tensions within the Wagner family, warring descendants of Wieland and Wolfgang, the two grandsons (whilst a student I had met at a concert of music by the Renaissance composer Josquin des Pres at the Brompton Oratory in London, Wagner's grand-daughter Friedelind, Nike's aunt, who had long since broken away from that poisonous atmosphere).

We had memorable conversations, usually over coffee, but once in the halfway decent restaurant in the Beethovenhalle, and it was there that I told her that Liszt's Piano Sonata was the greatest ever written (which it is), and in doing so made of her a friend for life. I think she was more proud of Liszt (information about him just spilled out of her) than of Wagner, with whom I suspected she felt a certain embarrassment.

I had grown to love Bonn very much, and to treasure all the performers I had met, and some of them interviewed there. I knew my way around the city, not least to an excellent Chinese restaurant and a cosy little chocolate cafe (the wrapper from a bar of their Beethoven chocolate is pinned to one of my study walls), and every time I went was like coming home.

But recent programmes ceased to be of interest to jaded old me, and at the time of writing, the coronavirus crisis has caused the cancellation of the two festivals which would have celebrated this 250th year of Beethoven's birth, and which would have marked Nike Wagner's departure in order to devote herself to writing.

I doubt I'll return to the Beethovenfest which had become so dear to me.

Opera in Russia

From the Irish Republic to the depths of Russia might seem a tenuous link, but it happened, thanks to the National Youth Orchestra of Ireland.

That amazing ensemble of youngsters was due to perform nothing less than Wagner's Ring cycle at Symphony Hall in Birmingham, after giving it in Limerick, and I was invited to go over to Ireland to write a preview.

When I arrived, after touching down from the Birmingham to Boston flight on a plane which seemed as palatial as an ocean-going liner, they were rehearsing for a concert conducted by the Russian Alexander Anissimov, who would be conducting the Ring. The youngsters' committee entertained me to tea, and I interviewed them. The concert was a huge success, and afterwards I returned to my hotel in Limerick, as did many of the musicians, to celebrate in the bar.

Early next morning I heard a knock on my bedroom door. I ignored it. About five minutes later the knock came again, more forcefully. I put on my long leather coat (I had no nightwear) and answered the door. A detective from the Irish Garda entered.

A young lady from the hotel staff had been murdered in the kitchens early that morning, and could I tell them anything? I told the officer that I had been in the bar at the end of the previous evening and had then gone to bed. He thanked me politely and that was that. But they were having to interview the occupants of every room in that large hotel and were doing a tremendous job.

As did the hotel staff, for when I descended, ready to leave, there were trolleys with coffee-urns and snacks for breakfast, even though the kitchen where the atrocity had happened was obviously out of action. Many of the NYOI members were there in a state of shock, as they had known the poor girl. What a horrible way to end what had begun as a glittering weekend.

The Ring they brought to Birmingham was a triumph, professional singers performing with them (not least lovely Suzanne Murphy as Fricka) so complimentary as to the young musicians' prowess. And how often do you actually get the six harps Wagner demanded? Three of them came from one family. Just think what an expense that was, in terms of purchase, maintenance and porterage.

Alexander Anissimov and I had become quite friendly. He was music director of Rostov-on-Don Opera, deep down in Russia near the northeastern gateway to the Black Sea, and his company was due to make a tour of the UK, including a residency at the chocolate-box Grand Theatre in Wolverhampton. I was invited to go over to Rostov for a preview.

My flight to Vienna was the first of the day from Heathrow Airport, but it was delayed. Consequently we landed late in Vienna, where I was to catch the ongoing flight. I was allowed to disembark first (thank goodness I only had hand-baggage, unlike my first trip to Bergen), and as I ran through the terminal I could hear the Tannoy calling for Christopher Morley to go to the departure gate for Rostov-on-Don, as the flight was about to leave.

My suitcase and I barged our way through the crowds, I jumped the queue at the security scanner, and there at the gate was a bus waiting for little me. We reached the plane, which was already on the take-off runway, with the mounting steps in position for me. I scrambled up them, even had the nerve to grab a newspaper from the rack inside, and took my seat.

I was on my way to Russia for the first time. The meal served onboard was a delicious goulash, and we arrived at Rostov in the middle of the afternoon. I was frisked by security, including a machine-gun wielding soldier who found my little pill-box filled with Italian liquorice pellets (great if you get a sudden cough in concerts).

"Cocaaayne?" he asked. "No, you idiot," I replied (my actual words), "since when has cocaine been black?" Thankfully he had no English.

I was met by Larissa, press officer of Rostov Opera and driven to my hotel, the Don Quixote, just opposite the absolutely magnificent opera house which had been built for the company within the last ten years (the director was on very good terms with Vladimir Putin). She ensconced me in my very comfortable room and then I went across the road and into the opera-house, where Alexander was conducting an intensive rehearsal of Shostakovich's Katerina Ismailova, Lady Macbeth of Mstensk.

As soon as he realised I was there Alexander stopped the rehearsal, came out of the pit to give me a huge bear-hug, and then introduced me to the orchestra. The performance itself that evening was excellent, and then there was the post-opera supper in the green room. What riches, what brandy (even between each course), what wine, and what talk!

We were all served by Anatoly, the so-attentive major-domo there, and who looked after us so well (I made a point of bringing him a little present – a leather credit-card holder – on my subsequent visit to Rostov).

Next morning we had a little tour of the city, taking in a memorable visit to the market. Rostov was one of the junctions of the ancient Silk Road between China and the West, and this market has elements from all that history, herbs, spices and textiles. But it also has a teeming fish market (teeming indeed, because some of the unfortunate creatures were flopping around still alive), and there was a very contented kitten curled up on a chair next to one of the stalls. There were two Russian lady critics who had decided to take me under their wing, and they encouraged me to imbibe a yoghurt-based drink, full of bacteria no doubt, which would be good for me.

I was also interviewed at length by a writer from the local newspaper, Larissa interpreting (she had excellent English), and I told them how I'd been attracted to the city by its wonderful opera company and what great ambassadors they were abroad. I think that hit the spot, and the feature made an impressive spread.

Rostov is actually a beautiful city, with an atmospheric old town and a bustling commercial centre. It also has a dignified cathedral and I was impressed to see everyone who walked by, even teenage boys, stopping outside its doors to cross themselves (Russian Orthodox-style, of course).

My flight back home next day was at a disgustingly early time I didn't even know existed, but there was my loyal minder and interpreter to meet me and to take me to the airport for the flight to Moscow.

I'm sure there were chickens on that flight, and there were no bins above our heads, only netting. When we landed all the untaken seats fell forward and all the passengers, including a family brood headed by an earth-mother who looked like somebody out of Chekhov, applauded.

A bus took us to another of Moscow's airports, where I bought a tiny little set of babushka dolls as a take-home gift, and then I presented myself at check-in. My dear little leather suitcase which I had bought on Stourbridge market had expanded since my arrival, with the huge box of disgustingly sweet chocolates the Rostov people had given me, as well as a beautiful coffee-table book of photographs of old Rostov. The case was bulging, but I was still able to sweet-talk the rather formidable woman at the check-in desk to accept it as hand-luggage.

I was on my way home. My return invitation next year would prove equally memorable.

This time the flight from Heathrow was overnight, leaving at around 10.30pm BST and arriving in Moscow at around 6am Russian time. As an overnight flight it wasn't too bad, and I was met in Moscow by a nice young couple who drove me across the city to the airport with flights connecting to Rostov. The husband was something in arts promotion, and spoke decent English. His wife had no English at all, but communicated by stroking my hair affectionately, and blowing me a kiss as they dropped me off.

After I checked in I went to look at the departure board, and it was then that the Monty Python foot came crashing down from the heavens. My flight to Rostov was delayed by five hours! Apparently fog in Rostov was holding up the departure of the early-morning plane from there (obviously the one which had brought me to Moscow the previous year), and which would be taking us back there.

All that time to kill, and this was in the days before e-book readers. I sat in the bar at a time when I wouldn't be awake back home, sipping a refreshing and invigorating beer, and observed two ladies doing the traditional thing of putting a pinch of salt on their tongue and then downing a shot of vodka in one. I really can't remember how the hours passed, but pass they did, and eventually we took off for Rostov.

So I arrived five hours late, exhausted and crumpled in the stone-coloured linen suit I was wearing, and as soon as I stepped off the plane I was hit by the heat (hence the early-morning fog), such a difference from the early winter chill of my previous visit. Larissa was there to meet me, and we drove to the same hotel.

She informed me that everyone was waiting for me with lunch laid out in the green room, but I asked her to give my apologies as all I wanted to do at the moment was grab a sleep. I was so exhausted I didn't even undress and take a shower, I just wanted some shuteye.

But at 7pm that evening I was across the road and on the stage of the opera house, ready for a huge public launch of the company's season, several of the administrative bigwigs onstage alongside me. Larissa was of course the interpreter when it came to my turn.

"My dear friends," I began, to 2000 people in the auditorium, and in my mind I thanked Kurt Masur for the way he had welcomed us from the CBSO Chorus during that 1997 visit. I apologised for my crumpled appearance, and explained that I had only recently got off the plane from London, and what a pleasure it was to be back here. I think it went down pretty well.

What the performance was that night has escaped my memory, but there was the usual sumptuous dinner afterwards, and I presented the gentle Anatoly with his credit-card holder, which pleased him very much.

The Don Quixote hotel had a very impressive dining-area. You couldn't call it a room, because it covered all one floor above the foyer, and there was a spectacular vertical fountain on one of the walls. The breakfast buffet offered an awesome choice, and there was even red wine available. Not even I could contemplate drinking that at that time of day, but I was in awe of a couple of sturdy Russian blokes plonking glasses down for themselves.

It was a beautiful morning, sunny and hot, and the cruise down the Don which had been promised me sounded perfect. Vyacheslav Kuschev, the genial director of Rostov Opera, arrived outside the theatre bearing a basket of 100 crayfish and a few other goodies, there were also crates of beer, and somehow four of us – Vyacheslav, Alexander, Larissa and me – made our way down to the quayside and a privately-hired boat, crewed by a delightful husband-and-wife team.

Vyacheslav taught me how to crack open and peel a crayfish, and we got through all 100 as we cruised down the river towards the Sea of Azov, next to the Black Sea. We passed a dacha which Vyacheslav had built by hand himself (my admiration knew no bounds), and everyone took photographs. In addition to the crayfish were shrink-wrapped bags of, I think, whitebait preserved in oil, and they were the most delicious things I've ever eaten – but I don't know where to find them here in the UK and I don't even know what they're called.

Next morning was the early flight again, and this time I was escorted by the crayfish trio. Alexander even stood in the check-in queue for me, while I did some shopping.

That really was my farewell to Rostov-on-Don, but not to the crayfish trio, and certainly not to Alexander Anissimov.

Soon after that the Rostov Opera Company came on tour to the UK, and gave a couple of performances at the Grand in Wolverhampton. Maureen and I took Ken and Yvonne Maslen along, and we were treated like royalty, with a post-show photograph taken of the whole company sitting in the front few rows of the stalls, with the four of us in the places of honour, centre front. Ken and Yvonne were thrilled with that.

I invited the crayfish trio for lunch at La Galleria, the wonderful Italian restaurant on the bridge between Birmingham's Chamberlain Square and Centenary Square, and where I had enjoyed so many lunches (often with Ken) and suppers. I was on very good terms with Marcello Manca and his wife Kay, the owners, and if I ever asked for items which were not on the menu, such as spaghetti al aglio e olio or piccata di vitello, Marcello would have them cooked for me.

One of the lead singers in the company was in the party too, and the five of us had an enjoyable time. My Russian guests all signed my copy of Mikhail Sholokhov's epic novel *And Quiet Flows the Don*, which I finished reading, in Rostov, on September 17 2005, as I wrote into the book (I have its sequel, The Don Flows Down to the Sea, but have never read it, as I doubt nowadays I could do it justice).

By the time our lunch ended there were only two parties left in the restaurant, ours, and a table hosted by Marcello himself. He sent us over a tray of complimentary liqueurs, undoubtedly limoncello, and Russians and Italians parted as though they were old, old friends.

Alexander Anissimov was keen to conduct the CBSO, and I said I would see what I could do. I accordingly recommended him to Stephen Maddock, the CBSO's Chief Executive, who called me many months later to tell me that Sakari Oramo was ill, and what did I think about them asking Alexander to step in and conduct Shostakovich's 11th Symphony?

Of course I endorsed the idea, and Alexander was accordingly flown over. I interviewed him in the flat in Brindley Place that the orchestra rents for its visitors, and it was lovely to see him again.

The programme also included Britten's Lachrymae for Viola and Orchestra, a piece Alexander didn't know (interestingly, during his student days in Leningrad he had sung Britten's War Requiem under the composer's baton – a surprise for Britten as he visited the city). Michael Seal conducted Lachrymae, with Principal Viola Chris Yates the soloist.

Britten and Shostakovich in the same programme, what a pairing. Alexander's Shostakovich 11 was searingly powerful (this will never be a work on Classic FM's playlist), and he was invited back for a concert the next season.

That was a matinee, with a tea afterwards at the Hyatt Hotel for subscribers, where I interviewed him. It was going well anyway, but when I asked him about his memories of Shostakovich, it really took off, with his answer.

"He smoke, he watch football, he like women..."

I treasure three souvenirs of Alexander. Loving the three Tchaikovsky ballets, I wanted to own scores of all of them. The Sleeping Beauty is easily available in an Eulenburg miniature score, modestly priced, but scores of Nutcracker and Swan Lake can only be bought as conductor's scores costing at least £300 each, and this was in the early 2000s.

On my first visit to Rostov I mentioned to Alexander my desire to have this unobtainable score of the Nutcracker. Twenty-four hours later I was presented with a spirally-bound photocopy of Alexander's own score, with all his precious markings, which he had had his secretary prepare for me.

And the same thing happened next time with Swan Lake, and Alexander signed both of these scores to me. I've never had the inscriptions translated. Perhaps my Belarusian neighbour Oksana, she of the Balzams every time she goes back to Minsk, can do so for me next time she comes round with yet another plate of delicious cakes.

But the thing from Alexander I treasure most is a Christmas card, on which he had drawn a stave and written the opening melody of the Grand Pas de Deux from Act Two of Nutcracker, just a simple descending scale, but so eloquent as a message of artistic friendship.

St Petersburg

My other visit to Russia was also opera-based. The St Petersburg Mariinsky Theatre were bringing a Ring cycle to Birmingham Hippodrome, conducted by their king of charisma and seat-of-the-pants reliability Valery Gergiev, someone I had long admired, and who was a great late into the night drinking buddy of nice Andrew Jowett after every concert he conducted at Symphony Hall.

The Hippodrome commissioned me on very generous terms to write a preview of the forthcoming event, and that began with a trek down to the ghastly Barbican in London, where Gergiev was rehearsing a concert with his London Symphony Orchestra. He and I had a lovely interview, in which I think talk of football and Manchester United was quite prominent.

Then came the flight to St Petersburg to sample part of the Ring cycle at the Mariinsky Theatre itself. I was accommodated in a very comfortable hotel within walking distance of the theatre, and I had a very helpful cicerone who was chair of the Friends of the Mariinsky back home in England, Caroline, the partner of Mark Doust, one of the CBSO's bassists. She organised all my tickets and interviews, was there to interpret, but otherwise discreetly left me in peace.

That first night the opera was Siegfried, I'm afraid my least favourite of the tetralogy, and I was very tired. I enjoyed the interval buffet, not least the little slivers of bread topped with caviar (let no-one tell me they don't like caviar), but was feeling very sleepy, and I left before the end.

Next day I explored the area of St Petersburg around me: the churches, the square where the 1905 massacre had happened (depicted in Shostakovich's 11th Symphony), crossing the bridges on whose fences lovers had placed padlocks attesting to their undying devotion, and then crossing the bridge over the awesome Neva river, partly thawed but still partly frozen over as this winter ended. An optimist was fishing from the bridge.

I was also given a tour of the old Mariinsky Theatre, with its huge bell offstage used whenever they performed Mussorgsky's Boris Godunov. Awesome isn't the word.

I also interviewed one of the company's sopranos, and the amazing thing was that no-one knew who would be singing any particular role in the upcoming performance. Gergiev liked a football squad approach, having people on the bench to be summoned where necessary. This certainly kept people on their toes, but he had been known to bring in different singers for the same role as each act unfolded. He also had a squad of conductors lined up, to step in if he was otherwise engaged.

That night the opera was the concluding one of the cycle, Gotterdammerung, due to begin at 8pm. But, as was not unknown with Gergiev, it began a lot later. We had an interview scheduled for after the performance, so that interview in fact began well after midnight, with an entourage of lackeys scurrying around him like Nibelungs doing various tasks while he and I talked.

"Thank you for coming all the way from Birmingham," he began, and the charm was working its magic again.

When the Mariinsky brought this Ring cycle to Birmingham I obviously had guest tickets beside me to allocate. Maureen was somewhat immobile at that time with a hip problem so I invited Richard, my best friend of nearly half a century, to Rheingold. He was gobsmacked, and said he couldn't wait to find out what happened next!

He is chairman of the Worcestershire county drama festival, and whenever anyone complains of something going on too long he says, "listen, mate, I've sat through two-and-a-half hours of Rheingold and it seemed like ten minutes!"

His son Simon, my godson, was my guest for Walkure, my favourite opera of the cycle (though Rheingold is the most perfect). I was on my own for Siegfried, but Richard was again with me for Gotterdammerung.

During the long interval we went across to Big Wok, a wonderful Chinese buffet to which I had been introduced by a grateful Chinese student of mine at the Conservatoire (sadly, and inexplicably Big Wok is no longer there).

We returned for the last act of Gotterdammerung and Richard was hooked, and that is one of the greatest thrills of my life, the fact that my best friend had become so enthused with Wagner.

It was recently his 70th birthday, and I gave him the DVD box set of the amazing centenary Ring production directed by Patrice Chereau and conducted by Pierre Boulez. He's been using the coronavirus lockdown period to view it, act by act.

Japan

Very early in January 2017 I received a mysterious email from someone in Japan, offering me business-class flights and five-star hotel accommodation, plus a generous emolument, in order to assess the standard of symphony orchestras in that country for a fortnight in February.

With so many scams and phishing schemes going on I smelt a rat, and was inclined to bin it. But it had mentioned my friend and colleague Andrew Clements from the Guardian, so I emailed him to ask if he thought this invitation was kosher.

"Oh yes, Chris, go for it!" he replied. Apparently the Association of Japanese Symphony Orchestras was coming to the end of a three-year assessment project in which critics from the west were invited to assess Japanese orchestras. Andrew had gone the previous year, but was unable to make this, the final year, and he had kindly recommended me to go in his place.

So of course I did go for it. My hosts were so meticulous in their planning and preparation and sending me all the details, and somehow I was able to marshal all my non-existent scanning skills to send them an image of my passport. Everything was arranged.

My flight from Birmingham to Frankfurt was routine, but when I boarded the flight there to Tokyo, then it was wow! None of the countless planes I'd travelled on before had had a left turn in the entry cabin, but this one did, and a whole new world opened to me, my first experience of Business Class.

I was sharing a little pod with one other person (and we didn't intrude upon each other's privacy throughout the entire long flight), the seat extended into a bed, there was a generously-filled wash-bag and a pair of slippers, the inflight entertainment had so much to offer, and the drinks just kept coming and coming, as well as personally-cooked meals. Even during the night we were looked after, with stewards tiptoeing around with soft drinks for those of us who were awake.

My time-clock had gone totally out of the window, but they served us lunch before we landed in Tokyo, where I was met by Shoji Sato, an amazingly busy and efficient man who was masterminding the whole project, and whose inside knowledge of the classical music world was second to none. We also picked up Wolfgang Schaufler from Vienna, one of the trio of colleagues who would be working alongside me during the next near-fortnight.

During the taxi drive to our hotel Wolfgang and I bonded very well. When we arrived we were greeted by Hiroshi Kuwabara, General Manager of the Association of Japanese Orchestras, who gave us both envelopes each containing the equivalent of about £3,000 in Japanese Yen for our living expenses during our stay. I think I came back home with at least £1,000 unspent.

I went up to my room, which was staggering in its palatialness. In the bathroom there were toiletries I'd never found in western hotels (aftershave, as an example), the loo was one of those wonderful contraptions which warmed the seat and flushed you a bidet, and the mirror above the washbasin had a special panel in the centre which didn't mist over, whatever the heat in the room.

This was a Saturday, and when I went down to the restaurant and tucked into a lasagne (I felt at home with that – more later about Japanese food) I enjoyed people-watching, as locals had come into the hotel to enjoy an evening out, and the women were all wearing traditional kimonos.

Next day was the first assignment, an afternoon concert in the NHK Hall from the NHK Symphony Orchestra conducted by Paavo Jarvi (I had had lunch with him many years earlier on his appointment as Principal Guest Conductor of the CBSO). I descended into the lobby and met the American part of our quartet, Paul Pelkonen, who webmastered his own website based in New York.

Wolfgang must have made a different journey there, but eventually we were joined by the fourth member of our group, Christian Merlin from Paris, with whom I also was to get on very well.

The concert was interesting, we had a brief interview afterwards with Paavo Jarvi, who significantly told us it would take about two years to train the musicians to play with spontaneity. Then it was back to the hotel, where I tried a different restaurant that night, and that was equally acceptable.

Next day was free, so I decided to go on a walking exploration of Tokyo. Big mistake, as I was wearing a new pair of shoes I had scarcely broken in, and after a while my feet began to hurt (in fact, a couple of weeks after my return home, the nail came off my right big toe, so that's a yuck-factor for you; in fact that very event has just repeated itself as I write, three years later).

But I had a lovely time exploring the city, and I found a bookshop which had a shelf of books in English. Though I had my e-book reader I was desperate to buy to hold and turn over the pages of something in English, and here I found the novel Silence, by Shusaku Endo, which I recognised as having been turned into a much-acclaimed film by Martin Scorsese. Of course I bought it, and over the next few days devoured this story of the earliest Christian missionaries to Japan and the tortures they and their followers had to undergo. It is an unmissable novel.

On the next afternoon we had a heavy meeting with all kinds of representatives from many Japanese orchestras, of which there are 34, including 13 in Tokyo and four in Osaka. I collected so many business cards that I could have set up one of those games from my primary schooldays, where you put a cigarette card up against the wall and your opponent had to flick it over with one of theirs.

And next day we moved on, travelling first-class (our hosts and interpreters were in standard class) on a bullet train, each in our own seat socially-distanced for a bit of quiet time, with continual views of the snow-capped Mount Fuji, to our next destination, the nuclear bomb-devastated city of Hiroshima.

Hiroshima was such a moving experience. Everything has been reconstructed in such a calming way, and the few surviving buildings from that attack on August 6 1945 have been carefully preserved.

We went to an early-evening recital in the Peace Memorial Museum given on a piano which had miraculously come virtually unscathed through that nuclear holocaust (ironically it was an American piano, a Baldwin). Afterwards we had a presentation from local schoolchildren, all of them determined that such horrors should never happen in the world ever again, and they pressed on us drawings, poems and essays they had created. This was very, very emotional.

Next morning we had a tour of the museum, dedicated to the memory of that dreadful but necessary attack. Most striking of all was the enlarged photograph of a flight of steps into, I think, a bank, with the shadow of a man who had been obliterated by the bomb embossed into the concrete.

We learnt that it took some time, many weeks even, for people, especially children, to develop symptoms of radiation, but we also learnt, most humblingly, of the entire city's determination that this must never happen again.

After our tour we had a private press conference with one of the Museum directors, and what emerged from that was the message that there was no malevolence towards the USA which had unleashed this horror. "We did bad things as well," he said, quietly.

Yes, they did, but two generations later, just as in Germany, the paramount desire is to keep peace.

The concert that evening had its limitations, the Hiroshima Symphony Orchestra playing dutifully but soullessly under its Japanese conductor. The players did as they had been told during rehearsal, but there was no spontaneity in performance. "The whole performance needed much more personality projected from all involved," I wrote in my review for the AJSO.

Our hotel was actually connected to Hiroshima's railway station, though you were never disturbed by any train sounds, and after breakfast the following morning it was an easy matter to step onto the bullet taking us to our next destination, Fukuoka (careful at the back how you say that).

Fukuoka is a beautiful city, built on a lot of water, and its concert hall has a garden growing up its roof, just like the little recital hall at Grieg's house in Troldhaugen. I explored a little, did a bit of shopping, then realised I was hungry.

Much as I was enjoying my Japanese experience, I did have a problem with the food. Breakfasts were always delightful, with a choice of so many things, both western and oriental, including curries. Other meals were less easy.

Sushi is, in my opinion, fashionably over-rated, so that was a no-no. I enjoyed anything fried in tempura batter, and indeed anything that was offered me when we were being entertained, but choosing myself when out on my own was more difficult. Restaurants had little ceramic models of their dishes displayed in their windows, but it was impossible to tell what they actually were. I'm sure everything was delicious, but I like to know what I'm ordering, so for the only time in my life I was being decidedly wimpish (is that an oxymoron?) about food.

That lunchtime in Fukuoka I found a burger bar, and went for that. I had a hunger for fries, anyway, so at least that was satisfied, though the burger was neither here nor there. Finishing my meal, I emerged and strolled a few yards around the corner of the shopping-mall – and there was an Italian restaurant, proudly displaying a menu I could understand and could have walloped. I felt gutted.

I got back to the hotel to find Shoji Sato, our host, in a state of great agitation. He had had to settle my laundry bill at the hotel in Hiroshima which I had forgotten to pay, and could I now reimburse him? Of course I did, covered in embarrassment, but I think that was the only blot on my copybook throughout the whole trip.

That evening's concert had an interesting, Scottish-themed programme, beginning with Mendelssohn's Hebrides Overture, continuing with Bruch's Scottish Fantasy and ending with Mendelssohn's Scottish Symphony. UK orchestras will busk through the Overture with little or no rehearsal, but here its performance was tingling and alive under Shao-Chia Liu, a non-Japanese conductor. And the Scottish Symphony was tremendous, I have used the CD I was subsequently given of this performance in talks I have given about my Japanese trip.

It is paradoxical. I have heard Japanese conductors in the UK and Ireland (Tadaaki Otaka and Takuo Yuasa) who conduct with huge personality (Otaka is awesome in Elgar), but the ones who remain back home seem hidebound, and think robotic adherence to the markings in the score is all that matters. There was one exception whose conducting was a revelation, but he had worked extensively in Europe. More of him later.

We moved on to Osaka on yet another bullet train. The speed is unbelievable, yet you feel so safe on these trains. The logistics of boarding them, being told exactly where to stand on the platform and the door opens into your carriage, are extraordinary.

Immediately we went on to the very impressive Festival Hall for a Saturday afternoon concert of two of Shostakovich's most harrowing symphonies, numbers 11 ("the Year 1905") and 12 ("the Year 1917"), both detailing momentous events in Russian history. One of these works alone is taxing enough, but to sit through two would have been quite an ordeal.

Except that these performances from the Osaka Philharmonic Orchestra were extraordinary, all thanks to the conductor, Michi Inoue, a Japanese conductor who had worked extensively in Europe for many years until a cancer diagnosis had confined him to Japan for a long period of treatment and chemotherapy. He has never since wanted to put himself through the taxing journey to Europe, but how I wish he could be persuaded to come to conduct the CBSO.

These Shostakovich performances were gripping, energised and emotionally draining. And I've never seen wind players coming off the substitutes' bench after the interval as I did here, so exhausted were their colleagues who had been playing in the first half.

Our hotel in Osaka was the one used for visits by the Japanese Royal Family, and there was a separate lift which took them up to their apartment. Never mind them, my room was amazing. There were two bathrooms, one at each end, with more complimentary toiletries than I had seen even in previous days elsewhere in Japan. I still have some in my wash-bag, and I am reluctant to use and lose them.

The dining-room was a gift-house of breakfast goodies, and I used to enjoy reading the Japan Times, an excellent newspaper which was already spilling the beans about the eccentricities of the US President Donald J. Trump.

Osaka was really our last base in Japan, but we hopped from there on the Sunday to Kanazawa for an afternoon concert. From the station to our hotel was one minute, and from our hotel to the concert-hall was also one minute. As we checked into the hotel, a young sumo wrestler was checking out, with quite an adoring crowd around him.

In many ways this concert was the most revelatory of them all. It was a concert-performance by the Orchestra Ensemble Kanazawa of Rossini's Barber of Seville, with an excellent cast of soloists, and it proved the most enjoyable performance of Rossini I have ever heard. The conductor was Marc Minkowski, who seemed to relish participating in the action, so much so that much of the musical responsibility rested on the shoulders of Abigail Young, the Scottish concertmaster of what was actually an excellent chamber orchestra.

That evening our hosts invited us four critics for a farewell dinner. We climbed the stairs in a little backstreet restaurant, removed our shoes before we entered the room, and enjoyed what I'm sure was a delicious meal (though I ate very little), with speeches and toasts. As we walked back to the hotel I spotted a cat, my first in Japan, and that set a crown on the evening.

Next day we had lunch with invited members of the orchestra, and this is where everything fell into place. The orchestra had played the Rossini with so much verve, and here was the reason: 25% of the players were non-Japanese, part of the legal constitution of the orchestra when it was set up by its founder – and didn't it show!

Our fellow-lunchers around boxes of bento (Japanese takeaways a little rung higher than KFC buckets) were the leaders of the string sections: Abigail Young the concertmaster, a Japanese leading the second violins, a burly tattooed and ear-ringed Russian ex-soldier leading the violas (he was such a lovely, gentle man), a Croatian leading the cellos, and the most devastatingly attractive Bulgarian woman leading the double-basses. Our conversation was frank.

These section-leaders had no qualms about questioning conductors and discussing matters of interpretation and articulation, and therein lay the success of the orchestra, unlike all the other ensembles who just accepted the orders and obeyed them. The Kanazawa Orchestra was alive and vibrant, not merely an ensemble of automata, and this was because of the input of international experience. This was to be the crux of my (and indeed our) final assessment.

That afternoon we returned to our base in Osaka, and we critics entertained our hosts to a farewell meal in a semi-Italian restaurant (which pleased me). Next morning I treated myself to an expensive haircut in the hotel's barber-shop, ready for the afternoon's four-hour symposium in another of the city's concert-halls to the Japanese press.

This was quite an event. We four critics were sat at tables across the stage, plus Hiroshi Kuwabara as chairman, and we had simultaneous translators speaking into our earphones. Those women did a tremendous job, and had to hand over to a colleague after 15-minute stints of such intensive work.

For the first half of the symposium we had each been invited to speak for 15 minutes on a topic involving our home territories, and I was the one to kick off. I spoke about the CBSO (which I knew had a huge fan-base in Japan), its history, its conductors, its base in Symphony Hall. At the end of my talk I was thanked by the chairman for my 40 minutes!

After a break we then gave our assessments of what we had heard over our visit, and we put the message across very clearly that there needed to be more of an international recruitment into orchestral membership. This was difficult, of course, because there were so many students studying at Japanese conservatoires, but I think we made our point.

There were many questions and observations, and an amazing amount of knowledge displayed about western orchestras, and eventually we concluded, retiring to the green room where copious amounts of beer had been laid on for us, and where we were given CDs of those amazing Shostakovich performances under Michi Inoue.

We made our farewells on our bedroom corridor in the hotel at the end of the evening, as three of us had early starts back home next day. Wolfgang and I were the first away, and we had a comfortable time in the business-class departure lounge at Osaka airport, with sake and snacks, before our flight to Frankfurt.

That long flight was enlivened for me by watching the recently-released film Florence Foster Jenkins, that poor duped, deluded woman portrayed so brilliantly by Meryl Streep. We arrived at Frankfurt, where Wolfgang and I said our goodbyes (he, Christian and I kept in touch for a while afterwards over the books we were writing). There was a business class departure lounge there, but after that long flight I really couldn't do justice to anything on offer before the final leg to Birmingham.

Arriving at Birmingham I tumbled into a taxi, apologised to the driver for not wanting to make any conversation after such a long journey, and arrived home in the early evening. It was good to be back, but the cats treated me with disdain, with an air of "where the hell do you think you've been?" all over their faces.

Chapter 12

BITS ON THE SIDE

Eking out a freelance existence means having to embrace all kinds of activities in your career portfolio (something we always stress to the students at Royal Birmingham Conservatoire, and we enumerated 52 different skills needed for a young musician to establish a career nowadays).

And even as an old musician approaching the knacker's yard I am still taking on things other than reviewing and my rare forays nowadays into the teaching I so much enjoy at RBC.

I have written programme-notes and translated obscure lyric texts for many years, but my chief activity in that field nowadays is writing CD insert-notes for releases from the remarkable independent SOMM recording company, headed by the amazing, formidable Siva Oke.

Siva both nurtures rising young artists and cultivates established ones; it's not many labels who can boast Roderick Williams, Peter Donohoe and Jac van Steen on their listings, and it is a pleasure to work with her too in an advisory capacity.

In addition to my work with the Birmingham Post I am also Midlands correspondent for Opera Magazine and Musical Opinion, the latter edited by my indefatigably energetic friend Robert Matthew-Walker.

I first met Bob at the boozy press conference in Birmingham's International Convention Centre launching Stephannie Williams' month-long Discover Denmark festival, and caught up with him again many years later after the passing of Denby Richards, his predecessor as editor of Musical Opinion, who had instigated a regular Music in the Midlands column from me.

Like the Birmingham Post, Musical Opinion carries a lot of international clout (apparently it has subscribers in 54 countries, two of them in Tonga), and this continues to guarantee me entry into events everywhere – though the older I get, the more selective I am as to those events for which I wish to make myself available.

Bob is simply amazing. He once sent me a timetable of his working-day, and it includes two stints in the middle of the night. His chief love is composing (he was a pupil of Darius Milhaud, no less, one of the iconoclastic Les Six), and he tells me he composes in his head while queuing with his daily shopping at the supermarket checkout. He has nearly 200 opus numbers to his credit.

But he also edits two magazines, Musical Opinion and The Organ, and many of the book, music and CD reviews are written by himself. And he reviews concerts as well for the magazines.

Additionally he has a bewildering armful of books to his credit, ranging from an authoritative biography of Grieg, through "Muhammad Ali – his fights in the ring", Simon and Garfunkel (which Bob told me he wrote in a week, thanks to his strict regime), Havergal Brian, Elvis Presley, and Madonna, who apparently once planted an immense lipsticky kiss on his cheek in gratitude. Jilly Cooper did the same to me after my review of her very well-researched and perceptive novel Appassionata, whose first 30-odd pages are actually inspired by the ambience of Birmingham's Symphony Hall and Hyatt Hotel.

For a while I was also an assessor for Arts Council England, writing reports on the activities of various applicant organisations to let the gnomes back in London know whether they were worthy of support. I think you can already sense my feelings about the whole set-up.

The ACE keeps moving the goalposts, artistic organisations who should be spending their time planning and delivering performances are instead having to spend all their time tying themselves in knots before attempting to jump through the latest hoops, and the ACE's criteria seem more concerned about political correctness than the excellence of the artistic offer. The whole organisation seemed staffed by wet-behind-the-ears youngsters who were desperate to get themselves on the rungs of the arts administration ladder, and who had probably never had any experience of genuine artistic activity themselves.

The questionnaires I had to complete and return were a joke, the same questions reappearing in different sections of the pro forma but in slightly different wording. I made my contempt for the system very clear, and accordingly my invitations to assess were withdrawn after a year or so. I am still happy to endorse grant applications from societies approaching the ACE for funding, and am well aware how much effort it is costing these amateurs who just want to get on with the business of providing music to the public.

I also do the occasional broadcast on BBC Radio 3, such as when Sakari Oramo and Andris Nelsons conducted their final concerts with the CBSO. I remember Andris' farewell, when Tom Redmond was to interview me during the interval backstage at Symphony Hall. Unfortunately the first half of the concert over-ran, and Tom had less than half a minute for our interview, and he was mortified.

Yes, I was interviewed on important occasions like this, but I was never a regular broadcaster, and this was thanks to the machinations of someone who had inveigled his way into high echelons purely by bluster and bullshit. He was taken on by the Birmingham Post during my wilderness years, he began broadcasting first on local radio, later on Radio 3, thanks to his plummy Nicholas Parsons-sounding voice, and then became a big noise (no pun intended) on Danish Radio for some reason.

When the post of Chief Music Critic of the Birmingham Post was about to become vacant he had the gall to assume the succession would naturally come to him, and had business cards printed to that effect. And then I was chosen!

He never got over the fact that he was passed over in favour of me! He had a huge inferiority complex about his total lack of musical qualifications as compared with mine, his musical knowledge encompassed 250 years at the most, and he knew nothing about pre-baroque or contemporary music, and little about opera. But he did have a good record collection.

But this was the killer. One time in the Director's Lounge at Symphony Hall he condescendingly said to me, "Oh, Chris, I told the BBC many years ago they couldn't possibly use you because of your endearing little stammer."

Everyone I've told this story to, beginning with Maureen, has wanted to scratch the man's eyes out. And the BBC do still use me.

* * *

This is a gratuitous aside. As I write I am listening to the Peter Moores Foundation-sponsored Chandos CD recording of the Sadler's Wells 1968 production of Wagner's Mastersingers (in English), conducted by the great Reginald Goodall, and featuring Alberto Remedios as Walther and Norman Bailey's unforgettable Hans Sachs.

In 1968 I was in the second year of my BMus course at Birmingham, and Opera was one of the major studies for that year. We were to be booked as a party to see a major production in London, and the choice was between Tristan und Isolde at the Royal Opera House and Mastersingers at Sadler's Wells.

Tristan was the fashionable choice (we had had it drummed into us ad nauseam how influential an opera it was – that bloody opening chord which can resolve in four different directions), but there was nothing to see onstage. Whereas Mastersingers, I argued, had so much visual spectacle (and much more attractive music, was my subtext). And I won.

We all made our way to London. Donovan Brown in the Final Year, who lived in Worthing (he was a teetotaller who could get drunk on orange-juice at a party), drove Roland, Jonathan and me to Brighton, where we stayed for a couple of days (heaven knows how Mum accommodated three hulking young men, along with herself, Dad and Aldo in a compact bungalow), and then the four of us went up to Sadler's Wells.

There was a frisson even before the performance began, as it was announced that the tenor Alberto Remedios, who was receiving sensational reviews was unwell and a Canadian tenor, Connell Byrne, had been flown in from Germany to sing Walther.

Byrne did a fantastic job, but he knew the role only in German, so it was a macaronic situation (no, go and look the word up) until the wonderful Act Three scene between Walther and Hans Sachs, when Norman Bailey switched easily into German to allow the text and music to flow more naturally. That was so moving.

The rest of the performance progressed to a triumphant conclusion, and we awaited the appearance onstage of Reginald Goodall, who had controlled these near six hours with such an iron grip. A tiny, dishevelled figure with trousers too short for him shuffled shortsightedly onto the platform, and we all wept in amazement and gratitude.

Then came the journey back to Birmingham, which in those days was up the M1 and across the M45, and as Donovan's car drew up at traffic-lights in Coventry, there, alongside us was another car driven by one of our friends, carrying another group of our cohort back. That seemed to set the seal on a memorable evening.

A few nights later there was a party in the flat shared by a coven of four girls in the Music Department, and Mastersingers was being relayed on the radio (this very performance which is playing as I write). We had all been there just a few days earlier, so we all knew it.

And guess who clambered up on top of the battered old upright piano to conduct everyone in the finale...

*   *   *

Conducting was a great love of mine which had to go, once I was appointed as Chief Music Critic on the Birmingham Post. I was out reviewing virtually every evening, so could not commit to rehearsals with the operatic society any more, and it was the same with the Halesowen Orchestra.

I have, however, been tempted out of retirement three times, the first of which being an offer I simply could not refuse.

Ian Thompson, with whom I had worked for a short time at the operatic society, and who by the early 1990s had established himself as one of the finest directors on the Midlands amateur stage, had been approached by a Black Country businessman to direct a week-long run of a show he was keen to put on in order to raise funds for Ian Botham's leukaemia charity. The show was to be performed in the open air in the ruins of Dudley Castle, and would involve weekly rehearsals on a Sunday morning.

Thommo approached Maureen one evening after rehearsals (she was still assistant-producing at the operatic society), explained all this to her, and asked if I might possibly be interested. She replied that I was so busy reviewing concerts, but if any show could persuade me to take up the baton again it would be this one: West Side Story.

Given my adoration of Leonard Bernstein, this was a no-brainer, and the fact that rehearsals were on a Sunday morning meant no clash with reviewing. I had huge respect for Ian Thompson (and he used to call me "the boss"), my good friend John Bedford, who had led the orchestra for my school shows as well as at all the operatic societies with which I'd worked, would "fix" a brilliant orchestra, and the immensely capable Sheila Bratt with whom I'd worked so comfortably at GEC Operatic Society would be the rehearsal pianist. We also had an excellent choreographer with whom I'd worked at Cradley Heath Amateur Operatic Society (CHAOS).

Soloists from societies all across the Black Country and North Worcestershire came for audition on the first Sunday morning, and we assembled a very strong cast. Regular rehearsals began (always, of course, followed by a pint in the nearby pub), and the show built very well.

There was one little difficulty, however. This was not a long-established company in which everyone would be used to working with each other, this was a huge mix of egos, everyone a front-liner back in their own societies, and desperately trying to shoulder their way to the front here. Some of them didn't take to my rigorous approach, either. I think they were used to being flattered and smoothed-over by weak, emollient music directors back home, and couldn't cope with my stricter methods, whose bottom line was basically that communicating effectively to the paying audience was more important than the performers just indulging themselves onstage.

No matter, I was able to ride that, though I missed the warmth across the footlights I had always received from my own societies, and especially the kids at school. There was always the orchestra.

And what a fabulous band John had fixed for me! There were people I'd worked with many times before, but also people new to me, and we all gelled immediately at the band call, which to me was always the most important part of any build-up to a show.

West Side Story is a very difficult score. and such a joy when you bring it off successfully. I needed to plan the band call so that people could acclimatise themselves, adjust to each other (and to me), and tackle their parts confidently.

I have attended band calls which were quite simply a shambles, and displayed the musical incompetence of the character calling themselves music director – merely running through the score from start to finish. You do not launch a band call of Carousel with the demanding Carousel Waltz, you begin with something which virtually plays itself, such as "We had a real nice clambake".

So I planned the order of West Side Story movements to rehearse, beginning with the easy, one-in-a-bar "I feel Pretty", and continuing through until at last arriving at the Ballet, which is so demanding in its intricate time-signatures and cross-rhythms, and which we, unlike most amateur companies, delivered uncut. It was a brilliant band call, and I knew everything was going to be okay.

Except it rained all week of the run! Dudley Castle is an atmospheric venue for performance, after you have climbed your way up through the zoo, and I had seen a tremendous Yeomen of the Guard there (John Bedford leading, of course). But now it was soggy, unwelcoming, and a danger to performers and orchestra.

The stage was slippery for the dancers, so they were inhibited. We couldn't risk the rain falling on the musicians' instruments, so the orchestra was sent down into one of the dungeons, with banks of closed-circuit television screens in front of them so that they could see my every movement, up there in a makeshift marquee in order to be in immediate contact with the stage. The orchestra could see me, but I couldn't see the whites of their eyes, and the reassurance of knowing they were ready for their next cue. But we made it work.

This little striped marquee was like a fortune-teller's kiosk, or a Punch and Judy show at a fairground. It was quite lonely standing in there, conducting at the drenched stage and looking into the camera, hoping the band could see me.

But arriving in there on the penultimate, Friday night, I saw that someone had pinned a model of a loo-roll holder onto one of the inner sides (and in full view of the orchestra on their screens). It gave the place the appearance of a public convenience. I found out at the end of the evening that one of the lovely percussionists was responsible.

And on the last night he surpassed himself. Now, in my little kiosk, alongside the loo-roll was a model of a machine dispensing contraceptives...

Because of the appalling weather the production lost an awful lot of money. The audience was minimal and there had been the expense of my little kiosk, and even more so, the closed-circuit television equipment. What had been such a well-intentioned enterprise ended in near-bankruptcy for the philanthropist, who had to remortgage his house. And of course, none of us received our fees.

But I now could say I had successfully conducted Leonard Bernstein's masterpiece, and repaid a little of the debt I owed him after that wonderful evening in Venice all those years ago.

* * *

That was in 1992, and it was not until 2008 that I was persuaded out of retirement again, this time by John de la Cour, husband of my very dear and oldest friend Diana from Salzburg days.

When their son Elmley was born after a long delivery, many years previously, Diana had waspishly asked John, "So where's my Siegfried Idyll?" For those who don't know the story, the Siegfried Idyll was a miniature symphonic poem Wagner composed using motifs from his Ring opera Siegfried, and which he conducted, the orchestra standing on the staircase leading to Wagner's wife Cosima's bedroom, on Christmas morning 1870, her birthday and very soon after the birth of their son, Siegfried.

John was determined to put this omission right, and he organised a huge surprise party for Diana's 60th birthday in the village hall in Morchard Bishop, where they lived in Devon. Highlight of this party was to be a performance of the Siegfried Idyll conducted by me, but all the preparations had to be very hush-hush, and Diana knew nothing of what was happening, as John arranged for a friend of hers to invite her for an overnight stay miles away.

Meanwhile all the arrangements were hurriedly made. The hall was bedecked, the food and drink organised, and the scratch orchestra assembled for rehearsal. Leading the orchestra was Ulf, a long-time friend of John and Diana, and indeed Elmley's godfather. He was a regular violinist with the Berlin Philharmonic Orchestra and the Bayreuth Festival Orchestra, and I was going to be conducting him! John and I had supper with Ulf and his family at the local hostelry the previous evening, Diana safely packed away.

Come the Saturday afternoon we had only an hour to rehearse the Siegfried Idyll, and it all went remarkably well: a runthrough to get around the notes, then a proper rehearsal for articulation and dynamics, a bit of tidying-up and that was that. The trumpeter in the ensemble was Elmley, who was an expert percussionist with the National Youth Orchestra of Great Britain and an ex-chorister in Exeter Cathedral, but who had taught himself the trumpet in secret in order to participate in this performance.

The other surprise acts then rehearsed, including a magician who I seem to remember carried out some spinechilling illusions, and then it was time for the party.

Around 100 guests were sitting at the decorated trestle tables in the hall, the orchestra and I were assembled behind the curtain on the tiny stage, and everyone was awaiting Diana's arrival. The idea was that we would play the first few bars of the Idyll from behind the curtain, which would then open and a complete performance would follow.

But Diana was so gobsmacked by all these people assembled to celebrate her birthday that she circulated every table, greeting everyone, and it was only after she sat down that John was able to give me the signal to start.

You could sense Diana's amazement, and as she told me afterwards, when Elmley came in with his trumpet contribution, she thought "Good God, what's he doing there!" John's well-planned surprise was a huge success, and I really enjoyed the curry supper served afterwards.

A couple of months after that, Rachel Blackman, press officer of the CBSO and an excellent one, I might add, decided that it would be good for all the back-office staff to form themselves into an orchestra and for me to conduct them.

So one lunchtime we all got together at the CBSO Centre and had a go at Haydn's Symphony 100 "the Military". There was a motley crew of performers, including one young lady who was a brilliant flautist but had never played in an orchestra in her life, so didn't know about silent bars and listening for cues; an overloaded percussion section comprised of people who wanted to be involved but had no instruments (Stephen Newbould, administrator of Birmingham Contemporary Music Group, kept them under control); CBSO Chief Executive Stephen Maddock led the second violins, and one of my wonderful team of Heroes (as I call my assistant reviewers), Richard Bratby, leading the cellos.

We had an absolutely great time, first playing through, getting to know the notes and then an actual performance. The players of the CBSO were banned from attending, but I can honestly say, hand on heart, that I have conducted the CBSO ... staff orchestra.

Chapter 13

NOT THE FINALE

In addition to my 22 years of teaching at Royal Birmingham Conservatoire I had always as a music critic enjoyed a good working relationship with its Principals. I had also been appointed an Honorary Fellow in recognition of my work on behalf of musical life in Birmingham and beyond.

The Italians have an expression "il mondo e paese" (the world is a village), and that is certainly true of the world of music, not least in a tightly-woven community such as ours in the Midlands. We are all swimming in the same pond, and it's the bigger fish who respect each other's integrity and dedication. My dealings with top professional ensembles such as the CBSO, and top soloists, conductors and composers are always smooth and based on mutual trust and admiration. Unfortunately it's the smaller fry, unwilling to accept the constructive advice I give, who make the occasional ripple.

Anyway, as I was saying, I have always got on well with the Principals of Royal Birmingham Conservatoire, and in 2015 the elevation of the renowned cellist Julian Lloyd Webber to the position, replacing my good friend David Saint on his retirement, was to change my life, and take it over for two years.

Julian's was a brilliant appointment, coinciding too, with the imminent move of the Conservatoire from the about to be redeveloped Paradise Circus to Eastside, in what was rapidly becoming the city's Learning Quarter. All attention was focussed on what was happening at the once humbly-named Birmingham School of Music.

One morning that summer the great, the good and I assembled in one of Birmingham City University's new buildings on the campus for a reception (dry, he adds through gritted teeth) prior to trekking over to the site allocated for the Conservatoire building, where Julian would be cutting the first sod.

Julian, nice David Roberts (a high-up in BCU's teaching and administrative structure) and I bonded immediately, as we were all following on our phones England's contemptuous skittling of Australia's first innings in the Test Match at Trent Bridge. The actual business of the day seemed an anticlimax after that.

A few days later I received a mysterious invitation to a meeting with Julian at Paradise Circus, and David would be there too, and there came the commission.

Julian thought it would be appropriate to publish a properly-produced history of the Conservatoire to coincide with the move to the new premises, and he thought I should be the person to write it. David offered a generous fee, half of it up front, the rest on completion and had already secured a publisher. The magnificent new building was due to open in September 2017, so that was the notional publication date.

Of course I accepted. I had never written a book as such, and was beginning to think that my only literary legacy would be hundreds of thousands of words in ephemeral newsprint (now here I am almost at the end of another one). Contracts were drawn up and signed and I began my research, with a deadline for the end of January 2017.

I really enjoyed my work, first reading through the centenary history of the Birmingham School of Music written by its Vice-Principal David Brock, my very dear friend from University days (I was his best man), and sadly already no longer with us, and also turning again and again to the tremendous tome detailing so many of the institution's dealings down the years. John Smith, secretary of the then Birmingham Conservatoire Association the compiler.

There were meetings from time to time with the wonderful publishers Elliott and Thompson and their design team, with their editor Jennie Condell holding my hand along every step of the way, but eventually I realised I was amassing too much material and actually had to get down to the business of writing.

Things were flowing well, with a reasonably strict regime in Casa Morley, but my Japan trip interrupted proceedings, so that I don't think I was able to sign off the complete text until April 2017. Don't ask me about the nightmare of selecting and captioning images, though they all look stunning. E&T are such amazing publishers at this kind of thing.

The book was all set for publication in the early autumn of 2017, not long after the Conservatoire's new buildings had been opened and were in use, and then came the bombshell: the Queen had graciously agreed to add the prefix "Royal", so that now the biggest university music faculty in the country was to be known as the Royal Birmingham Conservatoire.

This meant stopping the presses so that appropriate alterations could be made within the text (I think Jennie and her team saw to most of that), and most spectacularly, to the cover of the book, and the title *Royal Birmingham Conservatoire – Inspiring Musicians since 1886*. But when it eventually appeared, just before Christmas and primed on Amazon, it looked fantastic: a coffee table-type publication which was a joy to handle, meticulously indexed, and something which I felt I had brought into the world after an 18-month pregnancy. The next few months actually felt very empty, but I was already engaged in literary activities elsewhere (more later).

Prince Edward, Earl of Wessex, Patron of the CBSO and of the Conservatoire, had insisted on writing his own preface to my book instead of having it ghost-written by me, and he had read through all the proofs. He wrote a really supportive couple of hundred words, and I was thrilled.

Early in 2018 he was invited to a concert at what was now the RBC, with a tour of the building beforehand, and there was a private reception afterwards. On the evening of the concert (which of course I was reviewing) I hung around at the subsequent public reception, hoping to catch him when he emerged and be introduced, but nothing happened. Just as I decided to leave, he appeared from the inner sanctum. I marched up to him, grabbed his hand, introduced myself and thanked him for his interest in my book.

"I couldn't have handled this visit without it," he said, and we walked down the staircase together, he to his limo, me to a taxi. I should be writing this from the Tower of London had the security guards been doing their job.

*   *   *

That particular literary enterprise had come to an end, but another one was just beginning, and bringing that to its triumphant conclusion has proved equally as satisfying.

Early in January 2017 I was contacted by Stephannie Williams, from whom I hadn't heard for a while, asking if we could meet in order for her to tell me about a concert she was planning to present in Birmingham Town Hall to raise funds for a bursary in memory of her husband Gwyn, who for many years had been a popular principal viola with the CBSO.

We met for lunch at Carluccio's in Brindley Place, and she told me of her plans. There were to be performers from the RBC, where Gwyn had taught, and Julian Lloyd Webber would be conducting some items. But there was also to be a huge contingent of established professionals, members of the CBSO and Bournemouth Symphony Orchestra (in which he had begun his professional career), and soloists who were regular performers on the Musical Festivals at Sea Steve had organised for so many years. Mike Seal, a long-time colleague of Gwyn's in the CBSO string section and now a sought-after conductor would be on the podium for works like the Vaughan Williams Serenade to Music, with an amazing 16-voice ensemble fixed by the mezzo-soprano Yvonne Howard. Philip Head, another long-time colleague of Gwyn's in the CBSO strings, was fixing the orchestra.

It promised to be a wonderful event, and as I had always enjoyed working so rewardingly with Steve and had always admired Gwyn as a player, I offered to write the programme-notes.

Eventually the programmes, with tributes to Gwyn (including a lovely one from Sir Simon Rattle), biographies of the performers, details of the bursary, and my notes went to the printers, and Steve and I had a happy couple of lunchtimes in the Mason's Arms in Wilmcote (her and Gwyn's local) checking the proofs.

The concert was a huge success both musically and financially, and there has been another one since, this time given at the RBC. Each time many members of the audience have come from the loyal supporters Steve has built up during her 35 years of Music Festivals at Sea, but also from music-lovers from the Midlands who, like me, have always admired Gwyn's work.

But something else was stirring. During our discussions Steve had come up with so many anecdotes about the performers she had worked with, and the artists she had represented, until it became obvious to me that she really needed to crystallise these memories in printed form.

It emerged that Richard Baker, BBC newsreader and music presenter, whose activities Steve had managed for very many years, had been of the same opinion. So we went for it.

Chapter after chapter of the book we decided to call *Beyond the Notes* were emailed between us, me suggesting the occasional amendment, Steve generally accepting them. So many memories were tumbling out, of her family life in Stratford, of Gwyn's work in Bournemouth and Birmingham, of the festivals Steve organised in Stratford, in London, and the two huge Nordic ones in Birmingham, the artists she had managed, and the Music Festivals at Sea she masterminded. Sometimes it was difficult to keep them (and her) under control.

I approached Elliott and Thompson as potential publishers, but they advised me to look more locally, one of the best pieces of advice I've ever had from anybody. Brewin Books of Studley, now based in Redditch, was an organisation whose publications I'd reviewed many times for the Birmingham Post, and the product was always of impeccable quality. They were particularly interested in material of local interest and Steve's book had it in spades: Stratford's Royal Shakespeare Theatre, CBSO, and Wilmcote village life, it was all there.

Lovely Alan Brewin snapped up the book and his son Alistair worked so diligently at setting it, gallerying the many images Steve and I sorted through, and presenting a virtually finished copy of the book, even during the coronavirus lockdown. Publication had been scheduled for May 2020, but as I write (early June 2020), we don't know when it's going to happen, but it will. And STOP PRESS on July 31, I collected the allocation of author's copies of this most beautiful Brewin publication and delivered them to Steve next day. Her joy was complete with this coming into existence of *Beyond the Notes*, soon to appear on bookshop shelves and in online catalogues.

I have been so thrilled to be able to give my advice during this gestation of Steve's memoirs, and now she is reciprocating during my writing of this volume.

*   *   *

Which is coming to completion as we continue in lockdown thanks to the coronavirus crisis (and I make no comment about the headless chickens posturing in their handling of it, though my motherland seems to have been doing so much better).

The lockdown has put a brutal temporary end to the celebrations of my beloved CBSO's centenary. So many mouthwatering programmes and new commissions had been planned by Stephen Maddock, Mirga Grazinyte-Tyla, Simon Halsey and the rest of the team, and they have all gone for nothing. What will rise out of these smouldering ashes nobody knows.

I hope still to be there to write about the return to life of the CBSO, but in many other respects I am winding down in my reviewing activities, partly because of my increasing age, but also because of the way the whole business of music criticism is going.

When I began, over half a century ago (okay, call me an old fart if you must), music criticism was an art-form in itself. It had its own disciplines, its own structures, its own rigours, not least those of objectivity and writing to a fixed amount of words.

Today it is a messy business, with so much online reviewing from unqualified wannabes, spewing out paragraph after paragraph of rubbish which is more about the saddoes writing it than about any well-defined critiquing of the event under consideration. And it goes on for hundreds and hundreds of words. No subeditor on a print newspaper would accept such extravagance, and www.midlandsmusicreviews, the website set up for me and my team of heroes by Mike Spencer and Linda Fowler, sticks to such rigours.

Sadly, hard-copy reviewing is dying, and so many music magazines, *Opera* and *Musical Opinion* excepted, have turned into comics. So yes, I am gradually retiring from reviewing, but not quite yet.

I will continue to be passionate about supporting the CBSO, and many other organisations aside, but nowadays only on my own terms.

But my interests are taking a different turn. Slowing down the treadmill of reviewing, I am moving to the other end of the food-chain, and taking an interest in the development of young performers.

So now I, together with Stephannie Williams, am following and helping to promote, the progress of certain artists at the onset of their careers. We are also working with established performers for particular events and recordings, with the collaboration of Siva Oke at SOMM. Our joint experience of the musical world adds up to well over a century of wisdom which we want to put at the service of this art-form in which we have both lived and breathed all our lives. Heaven knows, rebuilding the arts world once the pandemic crisis eventually comes to an end will be difficult enough and perhaps we, looking back over our own long careers with our varied experiences, can do something to assist in its revival.

At the end of a Confession comes penance and absolution. Is this new direction in my life a penance? If it is, it is a joyful, positive one, a feeling that penance is meant to provide. Absolution? Perhaps the knowledge that I have always used what talents I have to show how enriching music can be, to praise and encourage, to expose complacency and disdain for the public, and to enthuse about the wonderful creations which leap out from a few dots scrawled on five lines of manuscript paper.

I have written at least once in a review that Bach's Mass in B minor is one of the few offerings that Man could present to God on the Last Day which might justify our existence. I hope that by celebrating marvels such as that masterpiece I have done my own little bit, too.

INDEX